Secrets
Visible and Invisible

**By Catholic Teen Books
Authors:**

Corinna Turner
Cynthia T. Toney
Theresa Linden
Susan Peek
T. M. Gaouette
Carolyn Astfalk
Leslea Wahl

First Edition

Cover design by Theresa Linden and Corinna Turner
Edited by Cynthia T. Toney

The following short stories are the work of the individual authors. Their inclusion here does not imply endorsement either by Catholic Teen Books or its individual authors.

Visit CatholicTeenBooks.com for more
title and author information.

Manufactured in the United States of America

Collection Copyright © 2018 Catholic Teen Books

Library of Congress Control Number: 2018906010

ISBN-13: 978-0997971828
ISBN-10: 0997971827

Praise for *Secrets*

I knew I was in for some great reading when I picked up this collection. What I was not prepared for was how exceptional this collection was. Often when I read an anthology, there are a few great reads, some good reads and some okay reads. That was not the case this time. Every story was a remarkable story. Some of the stories were so good, I immediately went back and reread just that story. And then when I finished the book, I reread the whole thing again a few days later.

I have a great deal of respect for the seven authors who contributed to this series. And even more so after reading their pieces in this collection... For fans of any of the authors in this collection, you need to pick this book up to read their contribution. For readers who love remarkable stories, this collection is for you also. And if you want some great reads that are clean and are Catholic fiction, this is the book for you. This anthology is Amazing! (Full review on BookReviewsAndMore.ca)

Steven R. McEvoy, BookReviewsAndMore.ca

Seven Amazing Secrets: At a time when so much entertainment and fiction for teens is saturated with envy, lust, pride and other moral toxins, the book "Secrets: Visible and Invisible" is a powerful, and FUN-to-read, virtue-rich alternative.

The talented team of authors behind CatholicTeenBooks.com has created the perfect way for readers to enjoy a taste of fresh new fiction that satisfies a deep hunger in the teen soul.

Teens ...you need to get your Catholic parents, grandparents, or teachers to get this book for you. Really. You'll be glad you did.

Cathy Gilmore, Founder/Executive Director, VirtueWorksMedia.com

Featuring seven fabulous stories from top authors in Catholic teen fiction, Secrets *is as entertaining as it is relevant and thought-provoking. It's sure to capture your imagination, move your emotions, and stir your soul. Teens and adults alike are sure to enjoy the variety of tales, which are cleverly united by themes of secrets and faith. Packed with powerful, meaningful, memorable stories, this anthology is so good, you won't be able to keep* Secrets *to yourself!*

Therese Heckenkamp, Bestselling Author

This anthology of short stories for Catholic teenagers is a true literary treasure. It provides genres for every type of reader, each so well written that the reader is invited to fully escape into many different worlds and places. The short stories will take its readers to dystopian Europe, high school hallways, a city block in summer, and a soldier's medical ward in 16th-century Italy, just to name a few. The characters are diverse, exciting, relatable; their adventures are accessible, mysterious and enthralling. But within these different settings, there is one uniting comfort: God is always there, whether revealed in a desperate prayer to a guardian angel, through pure romantic love, the presence of Christian charity, men and women religious, or within the sacraments. The hope that comes through Catholicism and Jesus prevails in each vignette, and yet there are still heavy doses of drama, suspense and tactful violence. So if your teens seem totally spaced out and properly engrossed, take courage knowing their love of reading and their love of the faith are being fed through these beautiful stories.

Regina Lordan, Catholic News Service

~~~†~~~

DEDICATION

For Blessed Pier Giorgio Frassati, model of charity and patron of young adults, who once said, "When God is with us, we don't have to be afraid of anything." Thank you for proving that adventure and holiness go together.

"Verso l'alto! - To the Heights!"

CONTENTS

FOREWORD

by Mark Hart
Life Teen International

We call Him Savior, Teacher, Wonder Worker, and Lord. He is the Alpha and the Omega, the Bread of Life and the Light of the World. He is the Messiah, the Promised One, the Divine Physician...the Good Shepherd.

Jesus Christ is all of these titles and an endless list of more. Yet, there is one title that I've rarely – if ever – heard used to describe Jesus of Nazareth, and I feel it is a glaringly myopic omission on our part.

Almost never have I heard Jesus Christ described as "Master Storyteller," though He most certainly was.

Consider this: Jesus Christ could have chosen to teach us in a variety of ways. Certainly, the Second Person of the Trinity could have spoken with such high-minded profundity that even the most educated Pharisees would have been reduced to intellectual rubble. Of course, Christ could have preached sermons with theological depth so unmistakable that the great St. Thomas Aquinas would have seemed a blithering moron or babbling toddler in comparison. No, the fact that the God of the universe – the Son of Man – chose to employ storytelling (parables) as His primary teaching tool tells us a great deal. Everyone loves a good story and storytellers have filled the world with history and mystery from the dawn of time. It is in stories, perhaps more than anywhere else in creation, that we come face-to-face with our fallen nature, our quest for virtue and our sometimes-hidden potential for greatness.

There is power not only in the story but within those hearts brave enough to bare their souls upon the written page. To be clear, the words shared reveal more about the author's heart than mind. Look no further than the Bible. God is not only the Creator and Father, He is the "Author of Life" (Acts 3:15). When we lose sight of this fact, we lose the essence of the Gospel and, in truth, our place in God's story of redemption. He is the author of all of our stories.

As Pope Francis reminds us,

"So this love story began, a story that has gone on for so long, and is not yet ended. We, the women and men of the Church, we are in the middle of a love story: each of us is a link in this chain of love. And if we do not understand this, we have understood nothing of what the Church is."[1]

There's a reason that the Bible has been translated into every conceivable language (even Klingon for you *Star Trek* fans out there). There's a reason that, when Johannes Gutenberg—a Catholic—invented the printing press, his first print job was the Holy Bible. Stories bring us together and share truth in relatable and disarming ways.

Finding quality stories in the modern age can be difficult, though, as most of us are so overstimulated that

---

[1] Homily remarks, April 24, 2013, Vatican City, Catholic News Agency
http://www.catholicnewsagency.com/news/church-is-a-love-story-pope-francis-says/

prose can seem somewhat archaic if not accompanied by a flickering image glowing upon a screen. We need more options – more resources and outlets of truth and beauty that can enrapture the mind and stir the soul. How do we engage people who might know God only sparingly or, worse yet, who doubt the reliability of Sacred Scripture but are open to something a little less intense and more "digestible"? At sixteen I certainly wasn't ready (or able) to dive right into the Scriptures. I needed an intermediary step.

Sure, I'd heard the famous Bible stories growing up. Vacation Bible School gave me the basic gist of the kid-friendly classics—your David and Goliath, Noah's ark, Daniel and the lions' den, and at some point, Jesus' apparent healing of a leopard (imagine my surprise and relief years later when I realized it was a leper). These fanciful stories failed to inspire me during my crucial preteen and high-school years. The Bible just didn't pique my interest enough to motivate me to read it myself or retain anything I heard from the pulpit.

I can honestly say that I wish I'd had this book when I became a teenager. I wish I'd have had talented writers (as you'll read herein) who cared enough about their faith and worked hard enough at their craft that they wanted to put their gifts and talents "at the service of the Lord" (1 Peter 4:10).

The writers of this book are sharing a piece of themselves with us all. The stories are unique and well-crafted, capturing both mind and heart. Each story reveals something different about the human heart and our constant (though, often veiled) desire for truth and virtue. You'll find yourself connected to and invested in the characters. With every turn of the page, the Holy Spirit will draw you more deeply into the love and mercy of God.

In sharing their gifts and stories, they are glorifying God. As the great Catholic author J. R. R. Tolkien reminded us, "Fantasy remains a human right: we make in our measure and in our derivative mode, because we are made: and not only made, but made in the image and likeness of a Maker." Put more simply, we write and create because we are made in image and likeness *of a Creator*. We work at a craft (in this case, writing) because we are saved by a carpenter – by a Master Craftsman. We tell stories because our Redeemer is a Master Storyteller – and the story is the net by which we catch souls for the Kingdom.

I hope you enjoy this collection of short stories as much as I did and, upon reading them, my prayer is that the reality and truth of God's love will come more to life in your life.

Happy reading!

Mark Hart

Sinner, son, husband, father and an (eternally) aspiring Catholic writer

~~~✝~~~

For nothing is hid that shall not be made manifest,
nor anything secret that shall not be known
and come to light.
(Luke 8:17 RSV-CE)

Dystopian

THE UNDERAPPRECIATED VIRTUES OF RUSTY OLD BICYCLES
by Corinna Turner

Trees flashed past as I peddled, my bike thumping and jarring as it bounced over the branches littering the path. Last night's storm had been replaced by utter stillness, but it'd left its calling card, all right.

Squeak-creak-thud.

My mountain bike's ancient suspension and rusty frame complained as I successfully cleared yet another obstacle. I focused intently on the path just ahead. I didn't want to crash, and I really didn't want to write off my bike. It might have been made *waaaay* back in the early decades of the twenty-first century—okay, okay, it wasn't quite as old as *that*, but it *was* the only one I—

Whoa!

I skidded to a halt, a whisker from Bane's cracked mudguard. "Bane! A little warning!"

He jerked his head forward. "What, Margo, you think I should've tried to jump that? On this heap of scrap?"

Ah . . . a fallen tree blocked the trail. Quite a big one.

I checked my watch. "Look, we're in good time. Why don't we leave the bikes here before we totally wreck them, and hoof it the rest of the way?"

"Good plan."

We hid the bikes in an area of dense bushes and headed on up the path at an easy jog.

"It was wild last night," said Bane. "Did you see the lightning?"

"I was, uh, otherwise occupied." And what a lovely Mass it'd been. Safe and successful, too . . .

"Oh, Uncle Peter was there, right?"

"Yeah. *And* 'Cousin' Mark."

Bane shot me a grin. "You know, I really like him. He's cool."

"Uncle Peter's cool, too," I said loyally. Father Mark had been there only a month or two. I did like him a lot, though I couldn't help wondering if he'd ever been an assassin. Probably why Bane admired him, alas, despite the fact that the young priest had clearly turned his back on anything like that.

"Uncle Peter's a different *kind* of cool." Bane jumped over another fallen bough without breaking his stride. "Father Mark's like, *cool-cool*."

"Bane!" I shot him a scowl for using the dangerous title out loud. Come on! We were fourteen; we were old enough not to make slips like that.

He shrugged, but then pulled a face and spoke more penitently. "Yeah, sorry. I guess it's better to be careful. Do you want to give me the lunch?"

"I'm okay." I always insisted on carrying the rucksack with our sandwiches at least part of the way. Even though Bane was big for his age, and a guy to boot.

Bane sighed and rolled his eyes but said, "Did Sue invite you to her party?"

"What party?"

"Well, that answers that. I told her I had something else on, but she was like, oh, well, I haven't *really* fixed the date yet, so you might as well tell me when you're free. So I need to get *really* busy for the next little while. Can you help me think of some stuff to be busy with, 'cause otherwise, sorry, I'm going to lie."

I laughed, warmth spreading and filling my insides. *He isn't interested in Sue.* "The tourist season's just starting. We could wash cars like we did last year. Get you a new bike before yours really does fall apart."

"That's a good idea. Maybe we could . . ."

"Bane, shhh . . ."

He fell silent.

No, I'd not imagined it. "The train! It's really early!"

"We're nearly there, we can do it! Give me the lunch!"

I slipped off the rucksack and tossed it to him. We picked up the pace, leaping over obstacles, racing the train up the mountain.

If we missed it, our whole day would be ruined! Well . . . it certainly wouldn't go the way we'd spent all week planning. Riding all the way across the valley, up to the top of Kerris Crag, a long, leisurely picnic, a little bouldering, and catching the train all the way back in the evening. A perfect spring day. But only if we caught the train.

I pushed myself hard, determined not to let our day be spoiled, determined not to spoil it for Bane with my shorter legs and weaker muscles.

There . . . There were the tracks. Panting, we jogged to our usual concealing heap of rocks, and waited, trying to get our breath back. We wouldn't have long. The whine of the locomotive and rattle of train wheels were very close. We peeped out as it came in sight.

Yes, a massive, snub-nosed, fat locomotive. A heavy-goods train.

"Good," muttered Bane. "It's *early*."

Early was better. As opposed to being the previous train, running *late*. That would've been no use. Passenger trains were awkward to get onto, quite apart from the fact that there was always one passenger who would tell the conductor that two teenagers had just jumped on and climbed up to the roof. We'd learned *that* the hard way . . .

"Ready?" Bane bounced eagerly on his toes as the locomotive surged past us. "Hmm, it's a fast one. We'd better go."

Normally we'd have allowed the locomotive—and driver—to get further ahead before making a move. But the train must've been lightly loaded to move so quickly— or the locomotive was overkill, considering how huge it was. Harell's Pass was long and steep, and the train was slowed by its climb. But maybe not enough.

We slipped out from behind the rocks and headed for the tracks, sprinting hard. Catching a train that fast was going to be much tougher than usual.

I focused on the wagons, taking in their design, my eyes hunting for the ladders. I'd never seen this kind of wagon before. They were huge—square and blocky. They looked incredibly solid. And where were the blasted ladders?

Crack. Crack-crack.

The sharp retorts made me start. Branches on the tracks, breaking? Or something bigger . . . but something bigger could derail the train . . .

Bane grabbed me, shoving me back toward the forest. *"Run, Margo!"*

Crack-crack. Crack.

Having a derailing train roll over me was not high on my list of things to do that day, so I ran with him, or tried to. He kept pulling me to and fro, zig-zagging as though getting away fast wasn't so important as . . . as being hard to *hit*.

Finally, my idiot-brain identified the noise.

Gunshots. *Lethals.*

A huge wave of adrenaline swept over me and suddenly I was running twice as fast, zig-zagging without needing Bane to push me.

Crack. Crack.

This is soooo not our train, is it? Lord, help!

Crack.

Pain seared across my upper arm, a red hot trail. I stumbled from sheer shock, almost going down.

"*Margo?*" Bane yanked me upright, sounding panicked.

"I'm fine!" I accelerated again. We'd be back to the forest in a moment . . . nearly there . . . nearly . . .

Crack, crack, crack.

Nearly . . . There! Trees loomed around us. We ran on, though, until the sound of the train receding over the top of the pass had died away into the distance. Then we stopped and flopped down on the damp ground, gasping.

"*Early*, my foot," I panted. "Military train, right?"

"Yeah." Bane was pulling at my jacket, trying to get it off. "Are you alright? Let me see that."

"What? Oh . . ." My arm . . . it still hurt. I winced as I slipped out of the jacket, trying to keep my arm as still as I could. The upper sleeve of my light green top was dark and wet. That of my darker green jacket, too. Blood.

Bane shoved the bloodied lighter green fabric up, peering closely, and wiped gore away with the jacket. "I . . . I don't think it's serious." His fractionally 'too-dark' skin—which bothered his prejudiced parents so much— had gone unusually pale.

"Don't faint on me, Bane." I tried for light-hearted and only managed weak. "I'm . . . uh . . . feeling a trifle dizzy myself, truth be told."

"I'm not going to . . . What?" His hands were suddenly patting me down, checking for . . . other holes? "Do you hurt anywhere else?"

"No." My head really was swimming. I felt quite odd.

He peered at me closely, his hand feeling my forehead with considerably more well-meaning than expertise. "I think it must be shock. I mean, you just got *shot*." He gave a ragged, awe-struck laugh, drawing a feeble chuckle from me.

Lack of expertise or not, he was clearly right.

"I'm okay." I tried to take deep breaths. "I'm okay . . ." I peered at my arm. A long raw channel ran across the upper part, where the bullet had torn flesh away, but it wasn't really very big, even if it was bleeding quite messily.

Bane shrugged off his own jacket, then dragged off his shirt in one quick movement without stopping to unbutton it. Slipping the jacket back on over his t-shirt, he ruthlessly ripped the shirt into three long strips.

"Your mum's going to kill you," I mumbled.

"She missed her chance to do that years ago." Sarcasm didn't quite hide the thread of pain in his voice. "I was thoughtless enough to come out of the womb looking like *this*." He waved the cloth strips in a head to toe movement. "But, poor her, I was without any actual deformity that would make infanticide legal—and heaven forbid *she* should do anything *illegal*. So she's stuck with me, isn't she?"

My heart ached for him. *Thoughtless, Margo! Think before you open your mouth.* But I didn't have the energy to continue an all-too-familiar, all-too-painful conversation, and I'd nothing new to say. I just sat and let him doctor me, trying not to wince as the bandage tightened around my arm.

"That was one weird train." My head finally felt a bit

more normal. "What *were* those? Secure transport wagons or something? They didn't even have ladders."

Bane had an unfortunate passion for all things military—though his absolute abhorrence of the EuroGov made him a more likely candidate in a few years for the Resistance than the EuroArmy. Although, not if I had any say in it! Not that I wanted him to join the EuroArmy, of course. Unfortunately, he was beginning to hang out with older teens, members of the Young Resistance. Though if he'd actually been out with them, he'd kept quiet . . . which he might have done, knowing how I felt about it. A flicker of hurt and resentment tugged at my heart, but . . . well, it wasn't like I wasn't keeping things from him, too. Or rather, one thing. One deadly, vital thing.

But he probably knew what sort of train it had been . . .

His hands had gone still against my arm, the last knot still to be tied.

"Bane?"

"The train. They weren't transport wagons."

"They must've been *some* kind of—"

"Not military ones."

"It had soldiers on it, Bane."

Suddenly, he swore. Really swore. Bane was less clean-mouthed than I was, but he didn't use that word lightly.

"Bane? What's wrong?" Coldness prickled up my spine, even as my heart accelerated.

He tied off the bandage in a few quick, frantic movements, shoved my arms back into my jacket—pulling it onto me with little consideration for my bad arm—and dragged me to my feet. "Come on! We've got to get out of here. Right now!"

"What's wrong? They won't care about two train-jumping teens, even if it was a military—"

"It wasn't military! It was the nuclear waste train from Coldwell, blast it! So, come on!"

"The . . . Uh oh." I allowed him to drag me to a run without protest. "You think they're going to over-react?"

"I think they're probably going berserk right now, and you can bet an army helicopter will be here in . . . however many minutes it needs to get here. But not many. Not enough. So, come on! You really think they could tell we were teenagers? I think we've got hard proof they couldn't!"

If they *had* realized we were just poor-sighted teens trying to jump the wrong train, they'd most likely have fired only warning shots. My arm burned ominously. Bane was right, they had no idea we were teens. And even if they did, *that* train? They'd assume we were Young Resistance, for once taking part in some larger adult operation—how many nasty bombs could the Resistance make, with just a fraction of the load that train was carrying? Bane was right. The authorities would be freaking out, and I couldn't blame them. No one wanted the Resistance to rob that train, not even me. Not even Bane.

We ran. Bane made no allowance for my shorter stride, dragging me with him at a breakneck pace.

"Where . . . are . . . we . . . going?" I gasped.

"There's a set of little-known caves near Rayle's Pass. It's the only place I can think of that will block thermal imaging that won't get searched."

"Rayle's Pass . . . is a . . . long way, Bane."

"Yeah, but if we get far enough away from the scene of the crime it'll be harder for them to be sure we had anything to do with it."

He didn't sound too hopeful, though. I mean, one male, one female; black hair, brown hair; brown jacket, green jacket? *Check, check, check.* I didn't fancy our chances. But what else could we do?

We ran.

And ran.

And . . .

Bane skidded to a halt, listening. I heard it too. A faint, distant chattering sound. Like you heard on TV.

"Is that a—"

"Yes." Bane grabbed my arm. "Come on!"

We ran.

The chattering got louder, but not too quickly.

"Flying a . . . search pattern . . ." Even Bane was breathing hard now.

My legs were turning to jelly and I was losing track of where we were. *Please Lord, let us be nearly there.* "How much . . . further, Bane?"

"We're getting there. We're nearly to the Whitly Caves. We could duck in there . . . if the chopper comes too close. But we can't stop there. They're on every map—there's even a parking area! They'll get searched for sure."

"You really . . . think they're . . . going to . . . "

"If they sent a *chopper*, then they're going to send troops to search!"

Alas, once again, he was surely right. That noisy bird was burning through the British Department's defense budget as we spoke . . . ran . . . staggered. Well, I was staggering.

Bane shot me an anguished look. "Margo, you've *got to* keep going."

"I'm alright. I'm alright . . . " I forced myself to take stronger steps, forced myself on. Still, everything was becoming a blur. Run . . . run . . . run . . .

I stumbled right into Bane as he came to a sudden halt. "What?" I focused tiredly and saw a steep-sided ravine crossing our path. Earth sides, not rock. Not sheer, but it would take time to get down and up the other side.

"Wait . . . this will be quicker." Bane pulled me along to where a branch had fallen right across the gap. "Hmm, a bit skinny. I'll go first. If it'll hold me, it'll hold you." Before I could object, he'd leapt onto it and made a run for it, arms flung wide for balance. He jumped off at the other side and looked back at me. "Come on, Margo! Take it at a run, it's easier."

There had to be a little more 'run' left in me, surely? *Angel Margaret, my guardian dear, help!*

The distant helicopter grew a little louder.

I sprinted for the bough, trying to make my wobbly legs firm, spreading my arms—*ouch*—like a tightrope walker. Looking good . . . halfway . . .

Snap-crack.

A glimpse of Bane's dismayed face . . . sky . . . earth slopes. . . . bushes . . . tumbling, bouncing off that earth slope . . . boulder flashing past my head . . . flowers . . . and *yeowch!*

I lay for a moment, trying not to whimper, then pushed away from the big rock I'd landed against—bad arm first—and sat up dizzily. A thick bed of flowery bushes had—mostly—broken my fall. Delicate hanging flowers, some purple, some pink . . . fuchsias, weren't they called? They grew all along the bottom of the ravine. Weren't they a garden plant? What were they doing out here?

A trail of flying clods of mud, grass, and small stones marked Bane's descent into the ravine, almost as fast as mine but marginally more controlled. He fetched up at the bottom with one last thudding leap and fell to his knees beside me, squashing more fuchsias. "Are you okay? Did you hit your head?"

"No, I'm okay," I managed, though my head still spun and my arm still seared. "Just my arm—"

"Then we've *got* to move! The chopper's getting closer." He pulled me up, but my right ankle crumpled under me.

"Aaah!"

"Margo, what is it?"

"I've sprained my ankle." I stared up at the steep slope in dismay—determinedly tried to shift my weight onto my right . . . *Ouch.* "Ah, no! Bane, fetch me a stick or something. I can't get up there without one!"

That chopper really was getting closer.

Bane glanced around frantically, then shook his head. "There's no time! Come here." And he unceremoniously tipped me over his shoulder and straightened with a grunt.

"Bane! You can't . . . Look, you'd better leave me. Get out of here! They won't be that suspicious of one teenage girl, right?"

"Dead wrong! They're looking for one female, remember? Now shut up and just let me . . . " He fell silent as he began to scramble slowly, painstakingly up the ravine side, chest heaving under my weight, and that of the sandwiches I was squashing.

Even he must've been running out of energy, and it was clear he couldn't go that fast carrying me, so he set me back on my feet when we reached the top. Pulling my arm securely over his shoulders and wrapping his other arm around my waist, he anchored me to his side, turning himself into one large walking stick. "How's that? Can you walk?"

I managed a painful step or two. "Walk, yes. Run, I doubt it."

"Walk will have to do. We've got to get to Whitly Caves before that chopper."

We walked. Well, he walked and I limped. The chopper crept closer and closer. Then from further down the mountain came the sound of a vehicle on one of the forestry tracks. A large vehicle.

"Think that's a forestry vic?"

"Troop lorry." Bane walked even faster. Almost drag-carrying me, in fact.

"You sure?"

"Well, you can glimpse vics on that track usually, down there through the trees, but I can't spot this vic, can you? So it's camo-colored."

Yes, the forestry vehicles that worked the lower slopes and Fellest proper were all painted bright orange so they didn't accidentally fell trees onto one another.

"I'm more worried about the chopper." He was still hauling me along as fast as he could. "It'll take the soldiers some time to reach this elevation, searching as they go. But if that chopper so much as glimpses us in its thermal imaging, it'll be another matter."

Wouldn't it just. I couldn't help peering over my shoulder now and then. The chopper sounded *so* close. Normally I'd have been excited to see one for the first time in my life. But not right then.

The rotor-noise surged again as the chopper cleared yet another ridge. How many ridges could possibly be left? Bane swore, ducked down, and before I knew it, had me over his shoulder again. He took off up the path like a deer with wolves on its heels. A heavily laden deer. Yes, if they had thermal imaging they might well be able to see us before we could see them. Not good.

After a few hundred meters, dark rock walls loomed on each side, cavernously wide at first, but narrowing as Bane carried me a little further in. Finally! He set me carefully down on a handy boulder, worn smooth by many a resting tourist. The caves were empty, though. The season hadn't started properly yet.

"Now what?"

"Now . . . " Bane was leant over with his hands on his knees, panting. "Now, we wait . . . for that chopper . . . to clear off . . . and then . . . make a run . . . for Rayle's Pass. Hide properly . . . "

"The troops *might* not come this far out, right?"

"They'll be calculating how far a grown man could run, uninjured, not carrying someone, and then adding a margin for error. They may search as far as Rayle's Pass and they'll certainly search here. Let's hope the chopper clears off before they get—"

An immense sound filled the cavern, reverberating from wall to wall. Wind blasted into the cave.

"Down!" He dragged me over the back of the boulder, to the cave floor.

Thrumming—clattering—hissing. The sound was hard to describe, but I knew what it was. Air rushed around, eddying from wall to wall, and dust whipped everywhere. I squeezed my eyes closed, kept my head down and fiercely resisted the almost unbearable urge to peep out. Because I was pretty jolly sure that a fortune in aviation technology was hovering in the clearing outside the caves, pointing its sensors straight inside. I would *so* have loved to see it, but not enough to risk being shot, or charged with being Young Resistance and shut in a secure borstal. Or, heaven forbid, even being certified as unReformable and subjected to early Dismantling. Though surely to goodness they wouldn't do that for a first offense?

Bane's arm was around my shoulders, holding me down behind the nice thermal-imaging-proof boulder, and his chest pressed to my back so hard I could feel his heart pounding. If he *had* ever been out with the Young Resistance, he'd certainly never been caught. All the same, his record wasn't quite as clear as mine.

Oh, go away, go away noisy bird.

Why was it checking out this cave so thoroughly? *Please let them not have seen us go in.* The cave was the only obvious hiding place from thermal imaging; surely that was enough to account for their interest?

The sound was changing, growing again, then fading as the chopper rose into the air and gained height—or distance? Hard to know, but the sound faded back to a distant chatter.

Bane let out a big breath. "I've got a bad feeling about this." He helped me back onto the boulder. "I think they may have seen us come in here. But we can't do anything. Unless it clears off. And it's not clearing off." He listened for a few moments. "Nope. It's maintaining altitude nearby. We can't sneak past it. Oh, this is not good."

Were soldiers already heading in our direction? My stomach churned uncomfortably. What would they do with us? How serious would this be? It would all depend on whether we could convince them we'd made an honest mistake whilst engaging in the local, technically illicit, but commonplace teen 'sport' of train jumping—or if they insisted on believing we were Young Resistance aiding some larger, aborted attack on the nuclear waste train.

Surely the total lack of evidence of the latter would be obvious?

Bane sat beside me, slipped off the rucksack, opened it, and handed me a squished sandwich. "Tuck in."

"Seriously?"

"Yeah, seriously. We may as well make good use of the time. I don't know about you, but I'm feeling pretty whacked."

Too true. Mechanically, I bit into the sandwich, chewed with difficulty, and somehow managed to swallow. My mouth was dry with fear.

We got through half the sandwiches and the chopper was still waiting. We began to catch far-off noises, audible over the distant rotors. A twig snapping. A muffled oath. The soldiers were on their way up to us.

Should we stay, or try to make a run for it? But my ankle . . . and Bane wouldn't leave me.

My ankle.

I grabbed Bane's wrist. "Quick! Let's put the sandwiches out properly, like we're having a little picnic, not a care in the world. Get the cloth out! Get the juice and the apples." I was shoving my hands into the backpack even as I spoke, emptying it. "There . . . I'll spread these out. I need something to hide the blood . . . your jacket! Give it to me, then get down that hillside and ask those soldiers to come and help your poor friend who's hurt her ankle."

Bane's bewilderment gave way to grim understanding. "We're going to be caught, so we may as well act innocent,

instead of cowering like criminals. You're right. Here . . . "
He shoved his jacket into my hands and bounded to the
cave entrance.

Hang on a minute. What if they shot on sight?

"Wait! On second thought, *I* should go." I'd be less
threatening.

Bane just flipped a hand over his shoulder at me,
though he did take a good look around the clearing—fully
visible from the wide-mouthed cave—before going all the
way out. Once in the open, he walked confidently, though,
no hint of furtiveness. Oh, why did he have to be so big
and strong for his age? It'd been useful for getting out of
that ravine, no mistake, but now . . . Someone could easily
take him for fifteen, or even sixteen. If only he looked
twelve. Or even *obviously* fourteen . . .

Quickly, I dragged his brown jacket on over my green
one. It was loose enough to fit over the dressing. *Thank you,
Lord.* Blood seeped through the bandage, though. Hitting
that rock must've made it bleed more. Well, it would take
longer to soak onto a loose sleeve than a tight one. *Please,
God, let us be out of this before it comes through.*

I spread out the little picnic cloth over the boulder and
arranged the sandwiches, drinks, and things, all the time
listening like mad for the moment when the soldiers
spotted Bane. The already-eaten sandwiches were a
leaden, sick-inducing weight in my stomach.

"Hey! S'cuse me? Can you help?" Bane's voice
suddenly came to my ears, deliberately childish. Followed
by a sharp military bark of something I was pretty sure

was, "Hands up!"

"Oh, wow, is that a real gun?" Bane prattled right on. "Are you a soldier? You are! Wow! I'm glad you're here. My friend's hurt her ankle. Can you give us a ride?" Clever Bane, immediately slipping in that his friend was female. *Relax, chaps, there isn't another big brawny young lad lurking nearby.*

"Where is she?" the soldier was barking. "Show us."

"Oh, wow, there's loads of you! That's great! Come on, she's just up here in the cave. We thought we might as well have our picnic where people might come. I already carried her out of the ravine she fell in, you see, and I just don't think I can carry her any further. But you guys look really strong." Bane's hopeful tone made me smile, despite our desperate situation.

A radio crackled—the soldier was reporting in. "Sarge, we've got a youth here says he has a female friend in the cave with a bad ankle. Checking it out now."

The static-y response wasn't properly audible to me, but I caught the words 'careful' and 'Resistance . . .' coupled with a term that would've been better obscured by the static.

Heavy boots crunched, and I hastily picked up a sandwich as the best available non-threatening prop, making sure to have it half-way to my mouth as the soldiers came into sight.

"Wow!" I said in a deeply impressed tone, once they were within earshot. "Where did you find all *them*?"

"They were just down the slope a little way." Bane sat

back on the boulder. "I told you I heard someone."

"Well, sorry I didn't believe you."

"That's enough chit-chat," barked the soldier at the front, though he seemed to have relaxed a bit when he saw me. I looked my age. He made a gesture to the other men, who fanned out around the big cave, menacing boulders, and outcrops with their rifles until satisfied it was empty. Six more had remained outside, clearly to conduct a search of the surrounding outcrops.

The soldier's eyes were checking us over, though, lingering on our hair—black and brown—and my double layer of jackets—brown and green. Blast. "How old are you two?"

"Fourteen."

He grimaced slightly, then turned, a slight flicker of relief crossing his face.

More boots crunched, and a voice bellowed, "What 'ave you got, then?"

"Fourteen-year-olds, Sarge. Two of 'em."

"Fourteen, huh?" The sergeant stopped in front of us, his eyes performing the same inventory. "Kids. What you doing out 'ere, huh?"

"We were going to have a picnic," I answered. "But I went and fell down a ravine and sprained my ankle. We started hobbling back towards the main road but it was such hard work, when we got to the caves we thought we'd have our picnic and see if anyone turned up. Loads of tourists come here, you know."

"Not this early in the year, they don't."

Trying to look young and stupid, we simply shrugged.

"And where were you planning to 'ave that there picnic?" His eyes raked us shrewdly.

"Oh, we'd have, uh, found somewhere nice," said Bane.

"Ever 'eard of . . . train-jumping?"

"Yeah, lots of kids do it around here," said Bane, unhesitatingly. "At least once, anyway. Parents freak out about it, but it's not that dangerous, really. I mean, I suppose you *could* trip and go under the wheels, but if kids know what they're doing . . . Though some kids have had other problems. We, uh, even heard about some kids who tried to get on the wrong train. They actually got shot at by soldiers. Scared the life out of them. They won't be doing that again in a hurry."

My heart was pounding right in my throat, or so it felt. *Innocent picnickers* clearly wasn't going to wash, so I understood what Bane was doing, but I was still terrified.

"Oh, really?" The sergeant was still eyeing Bane very narrowly. "And when was that?"

"Oh, it was really *quite* recent."

"Was it, huh. Ever 'eard of . . . the Young Resistance?"

"Of course. They're in the newspapers sometimes. Mostly graffiti and stuff. Some of it's quite funny!"

The sergeant's lip twitched slightly, then firmed. "Know anyone in it?"

Bane shrugged. "Well, how'd you tell? I mean, they wouldn't let on, would they?"

The sergeant grimaced slightly. "Got your ID cards?"

"Not on us. We're only fourteen!"

"All right, what're your names?"

"Margaret Verrall." I'd a clean record, after all.

"You're not going to call my mum, are you?" said Bane. "She'll freak out if you call her! Think I'm in trouble."

"Is that common?"

"No! I mean, there's been the *odd* little thing, but I've never done anything *really* bad. I don't want to be locked up!"

Smiling slightly at these boyish protests, the sergeant lifted his radio. "Sir? We're up as far as the Whitly Caves, and we've found no Resistance terrorists."

The radio squawked an almost unintelligible query that included the word 'helicopter.'

"It's jus' two kids, sir, that's all. One with a twisted ankle."

The radio squawked some more, rather hysterically.

"Yes, sir," the sergeant said sourly, and he replaced it at his belt.

My heart began to pound again. The sergeant had clearly figured out the truth of the situation; but, unless I was mistaken, our fate was no longer in the sergeant's hands. Blast and botheration.

"Look lively!" bellowed the sergeant. "Lieutenant's on 'is way up."

Some of the soldiers who'd started sitting down on boulders and leaning their rifles against walls hastily reunited themselves with their weapons and got to their feet.

"Oh good." Bane was still trying to act as young as

possible. "If the lieutenant can give Margo a lift, she won't need to walk so far."

The sergeant just gave another sour smile. I was getting a bad feeling about the lieutenant.

To fill in the stressful wait, Bane and I began nibbling at our picnic again. We offered some to the soldiers, but they didn't seem to dare be caught eating when the lieutenant arrived. Finally another troop lorry—or the same one?—rumbled into sight outside and came to a halt. A figure with slightly fancier epaulettes than the sergeant got out of the cab and trod eagerly into the cave, as more soldiers leapt from the back and rushed in all directions. Securing the area? Well, securing it even more.

"Well done, Sergeant! That's two of them in the bag! There'll be a commendation in this, foiling an attack of this scale."

"Sir, we've found these two *children*—"

"Children, pull the other leg! Look at them. Practically adults. Young Resistance, no doubt about it! Lock them up and throw away the key, I say! Better still, dismantle them and be done with it. They'll never be useful members of society. I mean, attacking the *Coldwell* train! I should think they *will* throw the book at them. Full force of the law, make an example . . ."

An ice-cold prickle ran down my spine. Was he right? Would the apparent enormity of our supposed crime outweigh our clean—or comparatively clean—records? Would they simply categorize us as unReformable? I tried not to shiver. *Lord, I trust in You. Lord, I . . .* I swallowed hard. . . *I trust in You.* The familiar prayer was suddenly surprisingly hard to say.

"Sir," the sergeant said stiffly. "After questioning the suspects, it's my opinion that—"

"You don't have the pay grade to have an opinion, sergeant," retorted the lieutenant. "Look at them, they fit the description exactly."

"I've no doubt they tried to get on that there train, sir, but I'm quite certain that—"

"You're going to lose that commendation if you don't watch your cheek, Sergeant. Now, keep six men, and secure the terrorists until we're ready to move."

"Yes, sir."

The lieutenant headed out of the cave, shouting orders. Most of the soldiers spread out in a long line, and disappeared from sight. The truck roared away again, with a few men in the back.

"All right . . ." The sergeant settled heavily onto a nearby boulder. "We'll be waiting here until they're done searching. Could be hours. You may as well get comfortable."

I leant against Bane, starting to shiver properly. This really, really wasn't looking good.

Lord, help us. Angel Margaret, protect us. Angel Bane, you must've had lots of practice, get us out of this.

Time crept past, but we couldn't bring ourselves to eat the boiled sweets the soldiers eventually offered us. I caught Bane shooting a look around. Wondering if we should make a run for it? If they really were going to execute us, it could hardly make things worse. But if they weren't . . . Surely they wouldn't. Anyway, with my ankle, it was all academic. Bane wasn't going to leave me, and there was no way he could take me with him.

"Don't even think about it." The sergeant suddenly spoke to us. Or to Bane. "There're soldiers all over the place. And you know what's down there over that'a way, right?"

What was the other way? Something dangerous, clearly. I tried to picture exactly where we were. Oh.

"The Facility." Bane scowled. "They shoot anyone who goes near it."

"They do indeed." The sergeant sank back into a morose silence, so I just sat close to Bane and shivered even more.

The Facility. The place they took teenagers who failed their Sorting tests at age eighteen. Where they put them through an exercise program and then dismantled them for their organs, using them to cure all the 'perfect' people who'd passed. The place where they took Underground members, Resistance fighters, and criminals for execution in just the same way. Or priests like Uncle Peter and 'Cousin' Mark, for the worst punishment of all— dismantlement without the anesthetic everyone else got.

I shuddered. Because the thing I'd never told Bane, what I'd tried quite hard to hide, in fact, not only from everyone at school, but especially from him, was that I might not pass my Sorting. I was top of the class in most things, but not in Math. I worked five times as hard as anyone else to achieve a middling mark, but come my Sorting, I wouldn't have five times as much time to complete the test. I might end up in that very Facility, myself.

I wanted to tell Bane, so much. But I couldn't. If he knew there was a chance of me failing, he'd throw everything away, insist we run. And I couldn't run. It would put his life in danger, and quite aside from that, my parents were running a secret Mass center from our house. The hidden sanctuary *must not* be discovered.

"Do you think they *will* . . . make an example of them?" My ears pricked up as one of the soldiers lounging nearby muttered to the guy next to him.

"Dunno." The other soldier carried on chewing a bit of fern. "Sometimes they do make examples of Young Resistance. But half the time you almost get the feeling they'd rather not catch them. Not till they can be tried as adults and given what all Resistance rats deserve." He spat on the ground.

Most soldiers were just normal guys working to support their families, with no more love for the EuroGov than the next person, but their hatred of the Resistance was rather less ambiguous. No surprise.

"Well, throwing kids in lock-up for a bit of cheeky graffiti? Public hate it."

"They do more than that, sometimes."

"Yeah, but they *don't* hijack trains! They *don't!*"

"Shhh!" The second soldier shot a look at the sergeant. But the sergeant just looked more sour than ever.

Finally, after long hours of interminable waiting, the sergeant's radio bleeped. "We'll be finished soon. Order a secure transport van to take those terrorist brats to base for interrogation." The lieutenant sounded in just as bad a mood. Clearly they'd failed to turn up any of those adult co-conspirators of ours.

"Yes, sir." The sergeant spoke tonelessly. He selected another channel and arranged the van. Dread chilled my stomach as I listened. After that, he sat and stared at the radio for a few minutes, before finally selecting yet another channel. But he spoke so softly into it this time—softly and deferentially—that I couldn't catch any of what he said.

The soldiers sat around and stared glumly at the cave floor. Bane and I sat around glumly and stared at the cave floor. It was the Cave of Glum, in the heart of the Fellest, all too near the Facility of Death.

Then the small, secure transport van appeared, bumping to a halt in front of the cave. No side windows, grilles over the rear. I swallowed. Bane swallowed, too, looking around frantically again, but then he just slipped an arm around me and snuggled me closer. Sometimes, in dark, pathetic moments of unworthy doubt, I actually worried that he *did* realize I might fail Sorting, and he just pretended obliviousness so he wouldn't have to do anything. Now was not one of those moments.

Two soldiers opened the rear doors and looked out. "Here we are, Sarge. You want us to load them up?"

"Uh, no, we should wait for Lieutenant Bayliss. He'll want to . . . see them properly secured."

The soldiers looked faintly puzzled, but shrugged and climbed out to mingle with their comrades.

Uh-oh, another engine. Lieutenant Bayliss and his truck? What would Mum and Dad say when they heard I'd been arrested?

Oh no! The house wouldn't be searched, would it?

On *these* charges? Of course it would!

Oh, please, Lord, no! Surely I'd just fallen through ice — drowning in freezing horror. How many lives would our innocent little picnic claim? *How could this be happening?*

Wait, not the truck. A small army jeep came into sight, bombing merrily along. It performed a perfect handbrake turn that spun it off the track and brought it up exactly next to the transport van, facing the other way — drawing a few admiring whoops from the soldiers — and switched off its engine. A shaking corporal jumped out of the passenger seat, ran around, and opened the driver's door, out of which emerged a surprisingly young officer, considering he had even fancier epaulettes than Lieutenant Bayliss.

A nearby soldier sniggered. "Lieutenant-Colonel Wexford-Merrell's still terrorizing his drivers, I see."

The Lieutenant-Colonel strode over to where the sergeant had just come to rigid attention, and he glanced at Bane and me. "So, these are the Young Resistance terrorists Lieutenant Bayliss has been telling me so much about?"

"*My* exact words to Lieutenant Bayliss upon catching them were 'two kids.' Sir."

The Lieutenant-Colonel moved to stand in front of us, looking us up and down, Bane rather narrowly. His eyes also lingered on my arm.

I couldn't help looking at it myself. Uh-oh. The blood had soaked through!

"So . . . Margaret Verrall," he said finally. "Completely clean record. One complaint lodged by the Greater Fell Railway company eighteen months ago with the police— who ignored it—concerning you being apprehended on the roof of a passenger train in the company of a young man who, from the frightfully rude description given, was once again alongside you when you two appallingly short-sighted youngsters attempted to board the wrong train this morning. Am I correct?"

Bane and I exchanged a look. The Lieutenant-Colonel sounded so posh his father probably owned an entire stately home, but he had an air of competence and hardness that suggested his rank was not so empty as that might lead one to believe. He also—unless I was dangerously mistaken—was on our side. *Right, Lord?* Bane clearly thought the same. We both took a deep breath: "Yes, sir."

He gave a short nod. "Very good. We found your bicycles, half an hour ago, it so happens. We left them right where we found them. *They* are practically sufficient to clear you all by their lonesome. No Resistance cell would use vehicles of that decrepitude for any part of any operation whatsoever, let alone something of this magnitude. Right, enough of this. I am calling this whole fiasco off." He jerked a thumb at his jeep. "Climb in, before Lieutenant Bayliss comes and takes your names, and makes himself feel better by making you the first Salperton teens to actually be charged with train-jumping." He swung around to the transport van soldiers. "You men, return to base. Sergeant, wait here with your men for Lieutenant Bayliss."

"Yes, sir." The sergeant—and most of his squad, for that matter—seemed to be trying not to smile. Certainly it was the Cave of Glum no longer.

Bane was already helping me to hobble toward the jeep. The driver opened a rear door and Bane maneuvered me inside.

By the time Bane was in, the Lieutenant-Colonel was slipping into the driver's seat again, shooting a look back at us as his resigned-looking 'driver' settled into the passenger seat. "I will drop you home. Do not go to the hospital unless you really must."

Guessed it was a gunshot wound, hadn't he?

He'd already leaned out of the window to speak to the sergeant and his squaddies one last time. "Oh, and listen hard, you men. This girl in all probability gave a false name. So you will not repeat such unreliable information to Lieutenant Bayliss. Understood?"

A chorus of "yes, sir" and a few titters greeted this order. Then the Lieutenant-Colonel put the jeep in gear and his foot on the floor, and I was clutching Bane's hand and wondering if we were going to die after all.

Bane just grinned at me, the skunk. He was enjoying it!

Still, a hair-raising drive was a small price to pay for our freedom and our lives.

Thank you, Lieutenant-Colonel, Sergeant.
Thank you, Angel Margaret, Angel Bane.
Thank you, Lord.

If you'd like to know what happens to Margo and Bane after Margo fails her Sorting tests, you can find out in Corinna Turner's novel *I Am Margaret*. Or see what happens to her older brother Kyle when he goes on the run from the EuroGov, in the novella *Brothers*.

ABOUT THE AUTHOR

CORINNA TURNER is the author of the *I Am Margaret* series for young adults, as well as stand-alone works such as *Drive!* and *Elfling* (for teens) and *Someday* (for older teens and adults). All of her novels have received the Catholic Writers Guild Seal of Approval (except new releases for which the Seal may be in process). *Liberation* ('I Am Margaret' Book 3) was nominated for the Carnegie Medal Award 2016 and won 3rd place for 'Teen and Young Adult Fiction' in the Catholic Press Association 2016 Book Awards. *I Am Margaret* was one of two runners-up for the 'Teenage and Children's Fiction' Catholic Arts and Letters Award 2016.

Corinna Turner is a Lay Dominican with an MA in English from Oxford University, and lives in the UK. She has been writing since she was fourteen and likes strong protagonists with plenty of integrity. She used to have a Giant African Land Snail called Peter with a 6½" long shell—which is legal in the UK!—but now makes do with a cactus and a campervan. You can find out more at www.IAmMargaret.com.

Contemporary

RECREATION

by Cynthia T. Toney

The old lady's house was the eyesore of the neighborhood. That was saying a lot, considering it stood surrounded by others with paint peeling in scales and lawns littered with trash. One of the oldest neighborhoods in our south Louisiana town, it was home to my friend Darrell and me.

Tight friends through middle and high school, we wore out countless pairs of athletic shoes walking those scalding streets, mostly to and from the community recreation center in summertime. First morning of freedom after graduation, we headed to the rec center again like we did every summer.

"Elijah. There she is," Darrell whispered over my head, poking me in the ribs with the sharpest elbow I'd ever known. "Everybody says she's crazy."

I glanced at the white-haired woman sitting in a hard chair on the front porch. "So this is why we came this way instead of our usual? To see an old lady? And she doesn't look crazy to me. Just old." I stole a second glance. Her dark eyes met mine, and I couldn't shake the feeling that she continued to watch me as Darrell and I strolled past.

Darrell snorted. "She never says anything. Just stares at you." He bugged out his eyes to mock her. "Even if you speak or nod your head."

"That doesn't mean she's crazy." I flexed my fingers. Her skin color was lighter than mine, although my arms and legs had been darkened to brown by the sun. We had similar high cheekbones and eye shape. Could she be half Vietnamese like me?

"I wonder if she has any money stashed away in that shack," Darrell said under his breath.

I shot him a look. "Don't even think about it." I added seriousness to my warning by jutting my bottom teeth.

At the rec, Darrell and I stripped down to our swim trunks. Each summer, the pool not only kept us cool but also kept Darrell and me out of the kind of trouble some of our former friends had fallen into. I kept an eye on Darrell anyway. He had only his mom and younger brother at home and didn't go to church anywhere. I'd invited him to St. Matthew's a few times and for dinner with my family afterward. He'd accepted twice but probably to feed his stomach, not his spirit.

On our way back home, Darrell insisted we pass the old lady's house again. He was certain she'd do something crazy to prove him right.

She'd vacated the porch, so I scrutinized her house and yard for signs of crazy. Green mold covered the white painted siding several feet off the ground behind scraggly bushes and tall weeds that reached her darkened windows. A rusted mailbox sat crooked on top of a post that looked as if the next storm might blow it down. No trash lay in her yard like at the houses on either side, though.

A shiver ran through me, and I jerked my eyes toward the nearest window. She could've been standing in the dark at one of her windows watching me survey her property. She'd think we were out to rob her for sure.

I squinted but couldn't see beyond the grime covering the windowpanes. Poor old lady. If I had to look out at the world through that grime every day, I'd be awfully sad. But alone, how could she clean windows and do all the other chores around her house? *Mom and Dad, I won't let it be like that for you when you get old.*

In the evening after dinner, I propped up in bed to read from my Bible. It had been a while, with exams and graduation and all keeping me busy the past few weeks. I flipped through the New Testament and came across verse 6:2 in Galatians. "Carry each other's burdens, and in this way you will fulfill the law of Christ."

My heart raced as if the apostle Paul had spoken directly to me. I raised my head. What kind of burden did he mean? Were helping my parents and keeping Darrell out of trouble all the good for others Jesus intended for me to do? The old lady's image on her neglected porch flitted across my mind. For the first time, I wanted to ease a stranger's burden.

The next morning, I phoned Darrell and woke him up. "Mind if I meet you at the pool? I have some chores to do first." Not a lie.

Darrell grumbled but said okay.

I set out on foot an hour and a half early. Knowing Darrell, he'd take the shortcut instead of using the path by the old lady's house since I wasn't with him, but I wanted to allow plenty of time in case he didn't. He wouldn't understand what I needed to do or why.

I slowed my pace as I neared her house. She sat on her hard chair on the porch, gazing at the sky. Instead of stopping on the street to speak to her, I stepped to the sidewalk and placed both hands on her chain-link gate. It rattled and drew her attention toward me.

My mind stumbled, and I babbled, "Um, hi, ma'am. Excuse me. I, um . . ." Why hadn't I planned what to say?

She glared at me a few seconds, and then a sort of recognition lit her face. Like she finally noticed what I had noticed before.

Maybe she did have the same racial mix as me! I cracked a little smile.

"Have I seen you at church?" She leaned forward and squinted.

I felt like a bug under a magnifying glass. "Um, I don't know." I swallowed. "Saint Matthew's?"

She nodded. "Want some iced tea?" she asked in a small voice.

Her invitation startled me speechless, which was probably better than my brilliant attempts at conversation.

After a second, I found my voice again. "Yes, ma'am."

"Come in." She waved me forward.

"Thanks." I unlatched the gate and trotted up the short walk to her steps.

She pushed against the chair's arms as she rose from it. Smoothing her baggy grey t-shirt over black pants, she said, "I suppose you're not planning to rob me."

My face warmed, and I shook my head. "No, ma'am."

"That's good, because I don't keep money in the house."

"I don't blame you."

She turned her back on me, and we entered through an old wood front door that didn't hang straight on its hinges. The hinge at the top needed tightening.

"I could fix that door for you." When she turned her head to look, I pointed to the faulty hinge.

"That would be nice." A smile spread across her face for the first time, and she waddled into the kitchen.

Clean but faded and scratched furniture surrounded me in the living room. Should I sit? Without knowing what she expected of me, I waited standing up, taking in statues of saints and the Blessed Mother on tabletops and shelves. I was staring at a huge ornate crucifix on the wall when she returned with the tea.

I accepted one of two glasses in her outstretched hands.

She nodded at a sagging plaid sofa, and I gently sat down on one end of it. It creaked. I took a sip of tea and hoped the sofa would hold.

"Where's your friend?" She chose a nearby matching chair.

"You mean Darrell? I'm meeting him at the pool."

Although it wasn't necessary, I added, "At the recreation center." That was dumb. She would've known about the only public pool in town.

She raised her eyebrows, wrinkles erupting on her forehead. "Do you enjoy swimming? It's a wonderful sport."

I nodded as I swallowed more tea. "It's a good thing in the summer. I try to swim in the mornings before I go to work at the hardware store. I just graduated from high school."

"What will you do after the summer?" She sipped her tea.

"Community college. In two years, I plan to go to a university if my grades are good enough." Why was I sharing this personal stuff with her?

"What will you study?" She set her glass on the table next to her chair, as if to better concentrate on our conversation.

"Right now I think maybe architecture or construction engineering." I'd made a footstool for Mom out of scrap wood the hardware store provided.

She laughed, a light and musical sound. "You can start with my front door."

So I started with the front door. Then I moved on to cabinet doors and loose knobs and drawer handles. Then wobbly closet shelves.

It became a regular thing over the next few weeks, my helping Miss Vivian. It was our little secret, although each time I asked myself why it should be. Was I embarrassed for Darrell to know I was doing something nice for a stranger?

For yard work, I arrived two hours before I was supposed to meet Darrell at the pool, so I could shower at Miss Vivian's and change clothes. She helped keep my secret by washing my dirty yard clothes to use the next time. Soon her yard was free of weeds, the grass cut, and the shrubbery trimmed.

I didn't complain about being tired. I accepted the sandwiches and gallons of iced tea she served. And the cake. I came pretty close to asking Miss Vivian for an extra piece to take to Darrell, but then I'd have to tell him about her.

On the phone, Darrell got too curious about why I had so many chores to do each day before meeting him to swim.

"Are you punished? Come on. Fess up. What'd ya do?"

"Nothing. Everything's fine. I'll walk with you today."

We took the route past Miss Vivian's house without discussing it in advance, as though we'd always gone that way.

Darrell stopped short in front of her house and stared. "Look at that. Somebody finally cleaned up that lady's yard and cut the grass."

"Sometimes all it takes is somebody who's willing to help—" I snapped my mouth shut before her name slipped out.

He smirked and kept walking.

"Darrell, what'll you do when summer's over?"

He shrugged. "I dunno. Keep working at the Burger Palace? I'm not interested in community college. I wouldn't even know what to study."

I'd learned that the usual reason for Darrell not wanting to do something with me that cost money was his lack of cash. "If it's money you're worried about, it's easy to get a grant based on your family income."

He squinted into the distance and shrugged again. His mom couldn't have been earning enough money on her own to pay for his education, but maybe I'd hurt his feelings.

"What do you like to do—something you could get a certificate or degree for in a year or two—that would get you a good job when you finished?"

He scrunched his lips and shook his head. "It's dumb."

"Come on," I said softly. "What is it?"

He sighed. "I'd like to build cars."

All these years I'd known him, and he'd never told me that. "So, why don't you study welding or something in technical school? I could help you apply for financial aid like I got."

He finally looked me in the eye and nodded. "Okay. Are you still starting college in August like you said?"

"Yeah."

He grinned. "Look at us. Next thing you know, we'll be dating college girls. Maybe I'll see how much that old lady pays to get her yard done, so I can get fitted up real nice."

"Maybe you oughta build some muscle first by doing

your own yard."

He swiped my head with his open palm. Only I wasn't kidding.

Bleach and water and a scrub brush got the mold off the sides of Miss Vivian's house. I cleaned the windows inside and out until they sparkled in the sunlight. *The exterior of the house could use a paint job, but how would I keep house painting a secret from Darrell?*

"I'd like to paint your house, Miss Vivian, but I'd need to hire a helper."

Her eyes brightened. "I can pay a helper."

That evening, I called Darrell to come over. He was in for a surprise.

In my room, Darrell squinted at the mention of my plan. "How much is she gonna pay us?"

"She's gonna pay you. I'm doing it as a favor."

He took a long step back, crashing into my desk chair. "What? Are you crazy?"

"You use that word a lot. And no, I just want to be nice. She's got nobody to help her, and it doesn't look like she can afford to hire somebody to do everything she can't do herself."

"Wait a minute." He held up his hands, palms outward.

I clenched my teeth.

"Have you been doing all that stuff around her house? The yard work and all that?"

"Yes."

"For nothin'?" His jaw hung open.

I nodded and held my breath for Darrell's reaction.

"Sucker!"

I breathed again and held my head high. "It's called being generous."

Darrell sighed and glanced at me sideways. "Look, you're my friend, and I'll help you—help her—for nothing."

"Seriously?" A slow grin spread across my face.

"I can't let you make me look bad."

So it was Darrell who surprised me the most, instead of the other way around.

After we finished painting the exterior of the house and I accomplished more inside, Miss Vivian asked for less labor. When I thought about it, she hadn't actually asked for much to start with. Most of the projects had been my idea.

"I thought maybe we could do something different today." She held two fists in front of her, palms down.

I grinned. "Whatcha got there, Miss Vivian?"

She turned her wrists and uncurled her fingers, presenting rosary beads in each hand.

"Oh." I attended Mass as much as any Catholic teenage boy, but praying the rosary? That was for girls. Mom had long ago stopped trying to get me to pray the rosary with her at bedtime.

Miss Vivian handed me one of the rosaries, a brown one made of wooden beads. "This was my brother's."

I sighed. She looked like she had her heart set on praying together. "Okay. Where do we do this?"

"We should face the crucifix on that wall. Let's kneel in front of the sofa." She groaned as she lowered herself to her knees, using the sofa seat for support.

I got down on one knee and then the other.

"Besides praying for peace as Our Lady of Fatima asked us, what would you like to pray for?"

I took a deep breath and blew it out. "That Darrell stays out of trouble, and I get a college degree." But I had many things that needed praying about. What about my parents? I was so lucky to have them, and I should thank God each and every day for them. But it had been a long time— years—since I'd prayed daily. Did God send me to Miss Vivian to help her, or the other way around?

"Those are good intentions." She patted my arm. "I'm praying for guidance in making an important decision."

"Okay." Sounded like she had a secret, too. What could Miss Vivian have on her mind?

"Let's begin. In the name of the Father, and of the Son, and of the Holy Spirit."

So we prayed, "I believe in God, the Father Almighty, . . ." And we prayed at least twice a week for the rest of the month.

One morning, I arrived at Miss Vivian's freshly painted red door with my dad's old digital camera. I wanted my parents to see what I'd accomplished, and wouldn't Miss Vivian enjoy getting her picture taken with an actual camera? I'd have prints made for her to keep, with her posed in every room we'd fixed up—and outside, too. If only I'd thought to take some "before" photos.

All was quiet at the house. Usually I didn't even need to knock on the door. She'd open it as soon as I stepped up, like she'd been watching for me. I peered through one of the windows where the curtains were parted. She wasn't there.

Well, she had the right to go on an errand or something without telling me first, didn't she? Maybe it had something to do with the big decision she had to make.

I'd catch her next time. It would be nice to get to the pool early, anyway.

But she wasn't home the next time either. A week went by, and my summer break was near an end. I'd have to start classes soon. Maybe I'd check with one of her neighbors. Someone was bound to know where she was and when she was coming back. I knocked on a few doors but got no response.

The following day I noticed a sign in her yard, three houses in advance of getting there. "For Sale," it read, with a real estate company logo, an agent name, and a phone number on it. I knocked on the door of a neighbor whose car was parked in the driveway.

"Do you know where Miss Vivian is and if she's all right?" I pointed to her house.

The young mother holding a baby on her hip frowned. "I'm sorry, but that lady passed away."

My heart felt loose, like it did the first time I jumped

into the deep end of the pool. I took a backward step away from the neighbor's door. "Thank you," I mumbled, my voice shaking.

My heart sank into place like a rock, aching in my chest. How could she be dead? She never talked about being sick. Never complained. Why hadn't I asked about her health? She must've been old enough to be my grandma. I stomped and kicked the dirt in the neighbor's scrappy yard.

I walked to the rec center numb on the outside and sick in my gut. Miss Vivian had sneaked into my heart and become special to me, and I didn't even get to tell her goodbye.

Darrell was already swimming when I arrived at the pool. He got out and met me on the side. "Man, what's wrong? You look like you lost your best friend, and I know that can't be right." He grinned and wiped water from his eyes with his fingers.

"Miss Vivian died," I blurted. I swallowed, fighting tears. I'd never cried in front of Darrell and wasn't about to start at eighteen.

His mouth dropped open. "Oh, wow, that's terrible. I'm sorry."

I shook my head, unable to speak for fear of sobbing.

He gripped my shoulder. "Was she sick? She didn't seem sick or anything when I saw her."

"I don't know. I don't even know who to call to find out what happened. She never talked about any family except a brother, and I think he's dead."

"Do you want me to get dressed, or . . ." Darrell searched my face.

"No, thanks. Stay and swim. I think I'll go home and see if I can go into work early. Get my mind off of it." I turned back toward the locker room.

"Sure. Take it easy. I'll talk to you later." Darrell's words faded behind me.

That night, Darrell phoned me as I got ready for bed. "Hey, man, how're you doin'?"

"All right, I guess." I chipped at some of Miss Vivian's white house paint still stuck under a corner of a fingernail.

"Sorry, but I've got more bad news."

"What?" Not that it would matter, unless somebody else I knew had died.

"The pool's closing."

I huffed. "So? Summer's almost over."

"No, I mean for good."

I sat down. "Really? Why? It's been there as long as I can remember."

"Some rich person had been donating to keep it open, and they're not doing it anymore. 'Course, we won't be using it much longer, but . . ."

"Yeah, the other kids coming up in the neighborhood need it."

"To keep 'em outta trouble like it did for us." Darrell's voice held a softness that was new to me.

"Maybe somebody else will step up by next year and keep it open." And maybe I'd be that somebody one day, if

I got through college and earned some real money.

"Maybe." Darrell's voice brightened. "Hey, guess what? I got a check in the mail."

"Yeah?"

"Now don't freak out when I tell you who it's from."

"Okay." To my knowledge, nobody had ever sent Darrell a check for anything, not even for his birthday or Christmas.

"It's from Miss Vivian."

A sensation like electricity shot through my brain, and I couldn't speak.

"Hello?"

I blinked hard. "Sorry. I'm here."

"It's dated from right after we finished painting her house. Somebody must've mailed it for her later."

"That would make sense." So there was someone close to her, somewhere. If only I could find that person to ask some questions. Maybe I could call the real estate company selling her house?

"And get this. The check is for two hundred dollars!"

My body jerked, and envy oozed into my consciousness. That was a lot of money—more than I would've expected her to have. She paid him that kind of money after I worked so hard for free? And then had to go to work at my real job afterward?

I sighed. I didn't do it for the money, and Miss Vivian never twisted my arm to do any of those chores for her. I wanted to do them.

"Well?" Darrell sounded so happy, and he needed the

money more than I did.

"That's great, Darrell. I'm really glad for you, but I'm worn out. I gotta go."

"Sure, man. Can we go to the pool together tomorrow or the next day? One last time? Like old times."

"Yeah. We will. I'll talk to you in the morning."

The next morning, the doorbell woke me with a start.

Ugh. The angle the sun was shining through my window told me that Mom and Dad had already gone to work. I untangled myself from the covers and got up.

Yawning, I peered through a living room window. A guy in a black suit holding a briefcase stood on the front porch. A nice car was parked in front.

Probably harmless. I opened the door.

"Are you Elijah Brown?"

"Yeah. Can I help you?" I ran my hands over my face.

The man introduced himself and handed me a business card. "I'm the executor for the will of Miss Vivian Williams."

My eyebrows shot up. What did this have to do with me? I was fully awake at last.

He showed no emotion. "Do you have any ID to prove who you are?"

"I think so. Sure. Just a minute."

I returned with my last student ID and handed it to him.

He looked it over and handed it back. "That'll do. Thank you. May we sit down?"

"Yes, sir. Come in. Sorry, but I just woke up." I led him inside and showed him a chair.

He sat and unlatched his briefcase on his lap. "Did you know much about Miss Williams?"

I shook my head as I sat on the end of the sofa. "What happened to her? I asked around, but nobody knew."

The man's expression softened. "She wasn't feeling well one day and called an ambulance, but she passed away before they reached the hospital. Heart attack."

My stomach flipped. "Oh. That's awful." Poor Miss Vivian. All alone and having to call the ambulance herself. If only I could've been with her that day.

"She had no living family, but she remembered in her will the people who'd been good to her. She apparently thought you were one of them, and she wanted you to have this." He handed me a clear-front wooden box containing a silver medal on a ribbon.

Wait a second! "This is U.S. Nationals medal."

He nodded but kept a businesslike expression. "Yes, it is. For swimming."

My mouth gaped open as I removed and held the heavy, shiny thing. That weak little old lady had been a powerful swimmer? No wonder she was so interested in me going to the pool.

"She also wanted you to have this." He handed me a photograph.

A muscled young girl with dark hair and dark eyes smiled as she proudly wore the medal.

"Wow." I sniffed and wiped the corners of my eyes.

What d'ya know, Miss Vivian.

"And this." He held out a white envelope.

I took it and looked at him.

"Please open it."

I ripped the end open and slid out its contents. A check. The biggest check I'd ever seen or had ever hoped to see. One that would cover four years of college tuition and maybe a whole lot more.

Like keeping a pool open.

Characters that are diverse in color, culture, and physical abilities live in Cynthia Toney's novels and in her first published short story, "Recreation," part of the *Secrets* anthology. Elijah and his friend Darrell were inspired by teens of African and Vietnamese descent that grew up in Louisiana while the author lived there. Readers unfamiliar with the southern U.S. states may not be aware that the neighborhoods, towns, and cities are quite a mix of interesting cultures, more so than some other areas of the country with which she's become acquainted. In addition to teens of those origins, readers of Toney's fiction will find Italian immigrants, Latino characters, deaf teens, and—coming soon—Jewish teens.

ABOUT THE AUTHOR

CYNTHIA T. TONEY writes for preteens and teens because she wants them to know how wonderful, powerful, and valuable God made them. Her novels employ hope and humor to address some of the serious issues young people encounter.

Cynthia is the author of the *Bird Face* contemporary series, including *8 Notes to a Nobody*, *10 Steps to Girlfriend Status*, *6 Dates to Disaster*, and soon, *3 Things to Forget*. A coming-of-age historical, *The Other Side of Freedom*, is set in a 1920s farming community. Her novels have appeared on numerous Catholic bloggers' Top 5, 10, or 20 book lists and favorites lists. They have also been featured in *Catholic Teacher* magazine.

She is a member of the Catholic Writers Guild and whichever author association or writing guild is available in the state in which she might currently reside, which so far has stretched across the southern U.S. to Texas. She has a passion for rescuing dogs from animal shelters and lives with her husband and several canines. She loves hearing from readers, who can connect with her through her website, www.CynthiaTToney.com.

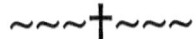

THE PORTRAIT OF THE FIRE STARTERS

by Theresa Linden

Five after seven, Caitlyn Summer clutched her purse strap to her shoulder and hiked up her long skirt. She raced down a hallway in St. Michael's High School. Late again. Why couldn't Mom get her anywhere on time? To get things moving faster, Caitlyn had even helped her younger sisters with their homework, fed her little brother a snack, and changed the baby's diaper. Mom and Dad had been deep in conversation about the budget and juggling the bills.

She turned a corner and glimpsed her destination, the teachers' lounge. The Catholic teen group, the Fire Starters, met there once or twice a week. Light—but no voices— came from the room. Strange. She usually heard them as soon as she stepped inside the school building, especially the loudmouths like Peter Brandt and his friends.

A boy's blond head peeked out of the room. *Peter Brandt.* "What, did you get lost on the way here? Hurry up, pokey!"

Caitlyn stuck out her tongue but not fast enough. He'd already disappeared into the room. Peter annoyed her like the older brother she'd never had, but then their families were so close they'd practically grown up together. Anyway . . . he probably couldn't wait to get the meeting started since they planned to talk about the upcoming camping trip.

Caitlyn picked up her pace. She didn't care what they discussed so long as Roland West was there. Not that they'd say much to each other. She typically spent most of her time talking to her friend Kiara and sneaking peeks at Roland, while he spoke either to his brother Keefe or to Peter. Sneaking glances at her.

Two figures stood at the end of the hallway, Father Carston and a boy Caitlyn had only seen in passing. Dressed in jeans and a wrinkled, untucked white button-front shirt, he slouched and stared at the floor while Father spoke to him. By his feet lay a bulging olive-green backpack, a weathered thing with frayed edges and an odd-shaped yellowish stain. She guessed the boy went to school here, but he didn't belong to the Fire Starters. A few of St. Michael's high school students did. The rest came from homeschooling families or attended River Run High.

"Maybe you'd enjoy it," Father said in a low voice.

"Really not my thing." The boy stooped for his backpack.

Nearing her destination, Caitlyn slowed, let her skirt fall into place, and combed her fingers through her hair. A few inches in, tangles stopped her hand, so she gave up. If she hadn't been in such a rush, she would've combed it before she left the house, or at least put it up. And she should've looked in a mirror. Roland might be here tonight.

She plunged through the doorway and —*smack*—right into a body. Her purse dropped to the floor, and something else crashed with a loud metallic sound. She stumbled back, her sneakers squeaking.

"Oh, sorry," she said. "I didn't mean to . . ."

The cleaning man stared at her through unusually round eyes, his head tilted to one side, something childlike in his manner. He signed something to her, making zeros with both hands and shaking them. Though she'd seen him around the school often—he was the assistant janitor—she'd never really looked at him. Tall and heavy, his chubby face didn't give away his age. He might've been in his twenties. Maybe younger.

The old metal trash can lay on its side on the floor behind him, a big black plastic bag at his feet.

"Can I help you?" Caitlyn stooped for her purse and grabbed the open side of the plastic bag, finding it half-full of trash. "I didn't mean to . . . I'm sorry."

He smiled, tapped his chin—maybe signing something—and took the bag from her.

"Oh, okay." Caitlyn bit her lip, not sure what he meant.

He signed something else but, just then, a girl on the opposite side of the room called Caitlyn's name.

Caitlyn turned, saw Kiara coming toward her, and

rushed past the cleaning man to greet her friend.

"You have to come see." Kiara's eyes were open so wide that the whites showed all around the irises. She grabbed Caitlyn's hand and dragged her toward the rest of the group, which included Roland in his black t-shirt and faded black jeans.

Her heart skipped a beat.

Roland stood with his back to her, staring at . . .

Her heart skipped more beats, her steps slowed, and red flags went up in her mind.

Everyone stood frozen in place, staring at the wall. Looking at what?

"Look," Kiara said in an awe-struck whisper, releasing Caitlyn's hand. "All the core members of the Fire Starters are in this picture."

"Really?" Caitlyn neared the group but still couldn't see it.

"It's a painting, not a picture." Dressed in animal-print pants and a striped orange shirt, Phoebe folded her arms and wandered a few feet from the group. Her no-nonsense attitude didn't match her typically eclectic wardrobe.

"What's the difference?" Peter turned toward Phoebe and must've glimpsed Caitlyn in his peripheral vision. He motioned her over. "Check it out."

Caitlyn pushed into the group. Her breath caught.

A three-foot-wide painting hung between windows. Several figures sat or stood in a room with couches, chairs, and windows that reminded Caitlyn of . . .

Caitlyn scanned the teachers' lounge. Three

mismatched couches, four armchairs, and several folding chairs sat arranged as if for two groups. A note on the coffee table read, "Leave the room as you found it." Evening sunlight poured in from the windows on one wall, shining on potted plants, bookshelves, and end tables.

The artist had painted this room with the furniture the way the Fire Starters had it for their meetings.

She studied the figures in the painting. They had no faces. One with sloppy yellow hair and a wise-guy pose reminded her of Peter and the way he gestured when he spoke. Two figures stood with him: a brown-skinned boy with jet black hair like Dominic's, and a boy with a humble, attentive posture that made her think of Keefe, one of Roland's older twin brothers. And there—

Caitlyn's mouth fell open. A skinny girl with long, messy red hair and a frumpy dress sat on the couch with another girl.

"Is that supposed to be me?" she said.

"Who else has a mop of red hair and wears outdated clothes?" Peter grinned, his eyes lit with mockery.

Caitlyn glanced at her long pink skirt. It resembled the one in the picture. "They're not outdated. They're vintage."

"Vintage. Right." Peter smirked. "I guess you could say that of everything you get from the second-hand store."

After shooting Peter a glare—he loved to taunt her— Caitlyn turned back to the painting and identified a few more figures. Where was Roland? She scanned the figures until she found one in a shadow.

Before she got a good look, Roland turned his pale face and gray eyes to her, as if he realized she'd searched for and found him in the painting.

Butterflies flitted in her stomach. She smiled and whispered, "Hi."

He gave her a nod and the hint of a smile, holding her gaze longer than usual.

Her heart melted and her head grew light as a helium balloon. She snapped her gaze back to his image in the painting.

"I guess that's me with you on the couch." Kiara took Caitlyn's hand again and giggled. They held hands in the painting, too, the way they often did when excited about something. "And there's Phoebe." Dropping Caitlyn's hand, Kiara pointed to a figure who sat on a windowsill in the painting. She wore a black vest, several bracelets, and jeans with flowered patches. Blue streaks ran through her fluffy hair.

Then Kiara turned her head.

Caitlyn followed Kiara's gaze to where Phoebe sat with folded arms and one leg swinging. On the windowsill. While very opinionated, she preferred to sit outside the group during the Fire Starters meetings. Unless Father asked her to sit with them on the furniture.

"Ha, look!" Peter jabbed a finger at the painting, his face brightening again. He must've found someone else to mock.

"Careful, it might be wet," Kiara said.

"It's not wet. It looks like it's acrylic." Caitlyn ran a finger over a lower part of the painting. A thicker stroke of paint dropped off to thinner paint that showed the crisscross pattern of the canvas, all of it dry.

Peter pointed again. "There's Roland." He turned a mocking face to Roland, who stood next to him. "Hiding in the shadows."

Roland shrugged and walked away, toward the couches in the middle of the room. The shyest member of their group, he did often sit or stand away from others.

Caitlyn admired his pale complexion and dark eyebrows and the wavy hair that hung over one side of his forehead —

Someone jabbed her arm with a sharp elbow.

"You paint with acrylic, no?" Dominic jutted his chin toward the painting. Then he tilted his head down toward her, his shiny black hair falling over his forehead. His new haircut kept it from covering his eyes. Now she could clearly see his hunger to uncover every little secret as he stared at her.

"Yes, but I didn't paint this. I'm not that good."

"Good?" Peter put his hands on his hips, bumping kids who stood near him. "They have no faces."

"So who did paint it?" Kiara glanced from one teen to another.

"And why?" Phoebe slid off the windowsill and stomped to the group. Arms still folded, she studied the painting. "I don't see the artist's name anywhere." She grabbed the painting, one hand on each side, and lifted it from the wall.

Several kids protested.

She turned the painting over. The canvas wrapped around a wooden frame with no markings. "Hmm. No name."

Peter pushed through the group, heading toward the furniture. The other guys followed, leaving only girls standing around the painting. First Peter, then the other boys began to slide the furniture into the arrangement the Fire Starters liked best, everything together and facing in. Scraping noises filled the air.

"What's the attraction, girls?"

The boys stopped moving furniture. Everyone turned to the speaker.

Eyes on the girls who stood around the painting, Father Carston strode to the little table near the kitchenette and set down a stack of books and a folder. A strange silence came over the room.

"Maybe Padre knows." Dominic clutched a seatback.

"Knows what?" Father approached the group of girls, who all shifted their gazes from him back to the mysterious painting.

The guys rejoined the group, everyone waiting in silence as Father studied the picture.

"Do you know who painted it?" Phoebe said.

Father gave Phoebe a strange look. "No, I don't. None of you know?"

The next week, Caitlyn arrived early, meeting the

cleaning man in the hallway instead of bumping into him inside the room. With a childlike smile, he signed something to her at the door.

"Thank you." She assumed he meant for her to go first, but he continued signing as she bounced into the room. Her mind boggled at the thought of trying to interpret his gestures.

"Come quick!" Kiara twirled her hand. The Fire Starters had gathered around the painting.

Not giving the cleaning man a second thought, Caitlyn rushed over. As she glimpsed the painting, her stomach flipped.

It had changed. The faceless figures sat and stood in the same places, but shadows indicated frowns and downcast eyes.

"All the people look sad," Kiara whispered.

Peter and Keefe backed up to let the cleaning man by— he signed something to them too—then they closed in on the painting.

"Wasn't the sky lighter outside?" Peter squinted one eye.

"Yeah, it was," Roland said.

"And your shadow's bigger." Peter smirked.

Roland elbowed him.

"So who is our mystery artist?" Dominic stepped outside the group and peered from face to face. "It must be one of us in this room, like a practical joke."

Caitlyn and several others turned to Peter, the best candidate for a practical joker award.

Peter's mouth fell open. Then he gave a crooked smile. "Yeah, right. You think I painted that?" He flung a hand out. "Now if something were rigged up to dump paint on kids as they walked through the door, I'd accuse me, too. But an actual painting? I'm all about stick figures." He turned a sly eye to Caitlyn, redirecting everyone's gaze. "Caitlyn's the only artist I know."

She wanted to shrink away. "I didn't paint that! I do landscapes and animals. I can't paint people any better than you can."

Everyone continued to stare, some of them through eyes narrowed to slits.

Caitlyn shook her head. What else could she say to prove her innocence?

"You paint." Dominic pinned Keefe with an accusing glare, and everyone turned to Keefe.

Caitlyn exhaled, relieved at the shift of attention.

"Don't you, *vato*?" Dominic called his friends *vato*, Spanish for *dude*, but his tone didn't sound too friendly. Neither did the way he edged into Keefe's space.

"Uh." Keefe's Adam's apple bobbed. "I paint abstracts."

"This is abstract." Phoebe folded her arms. "See? No faces."

"My work's way more abstract." Keefe glanced at Caitlyn as if calling on her as a witness.

Caitlyn shrugged. She'd seen a few of his abstract paintings, but it didn't mean he couldn't paint like this. "It's the same size canvas you use, isn't it?" She hadn't meant for it to sound like an accusation, but several kids nodded and whispered to each other. She'd only been thinking how she painted miniatures and he painted on larger canvases.

His face turned carnation pink. "Uh, yeah, I guess so. But I didn't . . ." He shook his head again, visibly unsettled.

Roland stepped forward and shoved his hands in his pockets, looking uncomfortable. "Keefe didn't paint that." Or was he looking guilty?

"How do you know?" someone asked.

"Because he said he didn't, and my brother doesn't lie."

Comments rose from the group, everyone challenging Roland.

"No, it's true," Caitlyn shouted above them. Her words had turned everyone against Keefe, so she needed to straighten things out. "I don't know a more honest person."

"How can he be so honest with a twin brother who is so dishonest?" A look of challenge glinted in Dominic's eyes.

"Hey, yeah," Peter said. "How do we know Jarret didn't sneak in here and paint this? In fact, I saw Jarret's hot red Chrysler 300 drive past St. Michael's just yesterday."

Keefe spun to face him and raised a hand as if to shove, but he stopped himself and ran his hand through his hair. "Leave Jarret out of it." He always came to his twin's defense, regardless of whether Jarret deserved it. "What reason could he have?"

"We all know he doesn't like us," Peter replied.

Keefe's jaw twitched, then his gaze shifted to Roland. And doubt flickered on Roland's face.

Caitlyn sucked in a breath. Yes, it could've been Jarret!

"Maybe you painted it." Phoebe jabbed a finger at Dominic. "You seem to like conflict. Maybe you wanted to see what secrets would come out from this. More gossip to spread."

"I take offense at your accusation," Dominic said. "Do *you* paint?"

"We all paint." Phoebe gestured to indicate the entire group. "We've all had art in school. Any of us could've painted this. So instead of trying to unveil the artist, we should try to find out what the painting means. Why no faces? And why do they look different today?"

Everyone turned back to the painting.

"Okay, so it's darker outside and everyone looks sad," Peter said.

"Right," Phoebe said. "Why did the painting change?"

"And what will it look like next week?" Keefe said, somewhat ominously.

Before anyone spoke again, Father breezed into the room. "Okay, group. Sorry I'm late."

No one replied. Other than Caitlyn, no one had taken their eyes off the painting.

A stack of folders and binders in his arms, Father stopped between a couch and the coffee table and scanned the room. "Did a new kid stop by?"

"A new kid?" Caitlyn scanned the room with him, discomfort prickling her skin at the unreasonable fear of finding a stranger hidden somewhere, someone she hadn't noticed upon first entering the room.

Finding no one, she took a breath.

Father's gaze found the painting and his head jerked back. "Looks different today, huh? That's interesting. I wonder—" He set his armful of folders down.

"What's this?" He lifted a sheet of paper from the coffee table. "Leave room as you found it. Put furniture back in place." He looked at the way the teens had arranged the furniture. "Okay, we can do that, right kids?"

The group broke away from the painting and straggled toward the furniture, a few of them mumbling less than enthusiastic replies.

Peter bumped Caitlyn as he passed. "They got a janitor. Let him do it."

"Yeah, isn't that his job?" Dominic said.

Caitlyn felt a twinge of guilt, but Mom always expected her to leave the Fire Starters meeting on time. She couldn't possibly hang around to rearrange the furniture. Before she took her seat, she scanned the room one last time. Who could've been watching them?

"Shall we get started?" Father clapped his hands together. "We've got a lot to talk about today."

"Bye!" Caitlyn slung her purse strap over her shoulder and opened the door of Mom's van. This was it! Roland had called them all together mid-week. Well, not all of them. Just the kids in the painting. Anxious to learn what he'd discovered, she jumped out of the van and slammed the door. As she turned toward the school, something tugged her skirt.

She glanced back and found her skirt caught in the door.

Mom gave her that knowing look through the window.

Caitlyn smiled as she cracked the door back open. "Oops. See you later."

"When your meeting's over, don't make me wait. I have an errand to run after I pick you up."

"Okay." A twinge of guilt pricked her conscience. Not only had she made Mom wait last time, talking too long with her friends, but she hadn't helped put the furniture back in order either. She hadn't even thought about it until just now. Surely, someone else took care of it.

Caitlyn turned and bolted up the steps to the school. She yanked open the door and darted into a dark hall, colliding with . . . someone.

"Oh, sorry." Caitlyn stumbled back.

A boy about her age stood before her. It was the same boy she'd seen around St. Michael's on Fire Starters' meeting nights. He rolled his eyes, hefted an olive-green backpack over one shoulder and walked around her.

"Sorry. Really." Burning with embarrassment, Caitlyn bit her lip and watched him go. Had he been talking to Father again? Father had seemed to want him to try something last time she saw them. Maybe he'd wanted the boy to join the Fire Starters.

She sighed and forced herself to walk, not run, down the hallway. Had Roland discovered the artist? Maybe it was the boy she'd just bumped into! Maybe Father Carston had talked with him to find out why he'd painted it. Could he have a reason for not liking their group? They welcomed everyone. Non-Catholic friends even came to their events sometimes. He could be a member if he wanted.

If Roland didn't know, they would have to investigate.

A burst of excitement tempted her to sprint the last stretch, but as she turned a corner, she gasped and put on the brakes.

Slow and steady, the janitor pushed a mop bucket toward her down the hall. His gaze connected with hers, and he stopped.

Glad she hadn't taken off running, Caitlyn waved "hello" and started to walk around him.

He opened his mouth and lifted a hand, as if he had something to say—or sign—but as she kept walking, he simply waved back.

A single voice traveled down the hallway, Peter hollering about something.

Kiara flew out of the Fire Starters' meeting room, her eyes wide open. "Oh good, you're here."

"What's the matter?" Caitlyn took Kiara by the arm and led her back into the room.

Halfway across the room, Kiara's arm went rigid and her gaze locked onto the painting. She stopped. "Look at our faces."

The guys stood studying the painting.

Caitlyn squeezed between Roland and Peter, who both

glanced at her. She meant to give them each a smile, but her gaze fell on the painting and her blood turned to ice. It had changed again. Tears ran down faces. Darker smudges had been painted where eyes and mouths should go. Night had fallen in the picture, and all the windows looked like dark mirrors that reflected eerie faces. It reminded her of Edvard Munch's famous painting, *The Scream.*

Caitlyn shuddered.

"Weird, huh?" Peter frowned.

Roland leaned behind Caitlyn and whispered something in Peter's ear. Peter mumbled back, and then he turned to the group. "Okay, let's all take a seat."

Caitlyn just realized that someone had arranged the couches around the painting. She sat on one end of her favorite couch. The one she sat on in the picture.

Her skin crawled. She should've sat somewhere else. Too late now. Kiara sat beside her and everyone else took seats.

"Couch, not windowsill." Peter gestured to Phoebe. "We need a group discussion."

She huffed, stomped into the arrangement, and plopped down on Kiara's other side.

Peter sat on the arm of a chair, the way Father often did. "Okay, so Roland snuck up here today—"

"I didn't sneak." Roland glared. "And I'll speak for myself."

"Oh really?" Peter smiled, seeming pleased to have annoyed him. He flung a palm up and slid into the armchair. "Okay, Detective Roland, speak for yourself."

Roland stood and sunk his hands into his pockets. "I wanted to check on the painting, so I came up here today. And I found that." He nodded toward the painting. "That's why I called everyone together. There's a message here, and I think we can figure it out."

"How do we know you didn't change it?" Dominic sat on one end of the second couch, next to Keefe.

Roland rolled his eyes. "I didn't touch it."

"We're not here to point fingers," Keefe said. "We're here to understand what it means."

Caitlyn pulled a notebook from her purse, dropping her lip balm and brush onto her lap. She dug for a pen.

"Right." Peter sat straighter. "So what've we got?"

"Well." Roland squinted at the painting. "First off, why don't the people have faces?"

Caitlyn jotted down "no faces" in her notebook.

"Maybe faces are too hard to paint. I could never do it," Dominic said.

"Is that why you left them off?" Phoebe smirked.

Dominic leaned forward. "Are you accusing me?"

Phoebe laughed.

"No one's accusing anyone." Roland lifted a hand. "We need ideas."

"Maybe there're no faces because the figures could be anyone." Kiara looked at Caitlyn while she spoke. "Maybe they aren't meant to be us, but we were the models."

Thinking the idea worthy, Caitlyn jotted it down in her notebook.

"You could be right." Caitlyn dropped her pen but resisted the urge to grab Kiara's hands. They would look just like they did in the picture. "But who's watching us often enough to use us as models?"

Roland glanced over his shoulder.

Peter looked too. "Okay, let's not get paranoid. What's the second point?"

"Why have they changed?" Roland said.

"Reminds me of *The Picture of Dorian Gray*," Keefe said.

"Dorian Gray?" Peter guffawed. "So that's a reflection of our souls?"

"That's not what the story means." Phoebe folded her arms.

"Oh, yeah?" Peter smacked the arms of his chair. "So what's it about? Why did the painting get uglier the more the dude sinned?"

"Oscar Wilde—that's the author—," Phoebe said, "was making a statement that the purpose of art is to have no purpose."

"So that's why he wrote the book, huh?" Peter let out a laugh. "Sounds like he had a purpose."

Phoebe shrugged. "He didn't want people thinking art was only for moral enlightenment."

"Art should have a purpose." Keefe bounced one leg and glanced around the room, maybe looking for someone to agree with him. "You ever see famous Italian works? They can really move you, make you think, lift your thoughts. Artists like Michelangelo, Botticelli, Da Vinci, and Raphael."

Caitlyn gave him a smile. He'd told her all about his trip to Italy with his father and the museums they'd visited. It sounded like quite an adventure.

"Are you talking about Ninja turtles?" Peter smirked. "We need to talk about *our* artist and *our* painting."

Mouth half open, Keefe shook his head. "Artwork, good books, they should have a message."

"So what's the message for us?" From her seat on the couch, Caitlyn studied the painting. "If we're all Dorian Gray, what are we doing wrong? It's been changing every time we see it, looking sadder and sadder."

"Okay, self-examination time." Peter stood and paced, rubbing his chin. "Who doesn't like us?"

Roland sat down next to Keefe, seeming content to let Peter take over the discussion.

"What is not to like?" Dominic said. "We pray together and we help people, like when we helped the Finns with their new house."

"And we do fun things," Kiara said. "Do we leave anyone out?"

"We leave out all kinds of people." Peter stopped pacing and spread his hands. "We're a teen group, so we leave out the young and the old. We're here in the Black Hills, so we leave out everyone else on the planet. And we're Catholic, so we leave out everyone of every other faith."

"We don't leave them out." Kiara sounded defensive. "They can come if they want."

"Well, we do Catholic-y things," Peter said.

"Well it's not like we're discriminating against anyone," Caitlyn said, in support of Kiara. "Besides, can't a group be for specific people?"

Roland gazed at the painting. "What about the time of day in the painting?"

Caitlyn looked from him to the dark windows in the painting. She shivered.

"It's darker outside every time we see it." Roland's gaze shifted to a window and he did a double take.

As Caitlyn turned to the window, she glimpsed a figure outside in the dwindling light. He dodged behind one of three parked cars in the church parking lot before she got a good look, but she did notice that he wore jeans, a white shirt, and a dark backpack. It must've been the same boy she'd seen before. Maybe she should tell the others about him.

"Right. Darker outside." Peter spun to the painting. "It started off in the evening, like when our group meets, but now it's pitch black. What comes next?"

"And our faces looked normal in the beginning," Kiara said, "but now we're all sad."

"Why are we sad?" Keefe asked. "Maybe the artist is sad."

"Maybe some psychopath is going to kidnap and torture us." Peter glanced at the group over his shoulder and waggled his brows. "And we're almost out of time."

"Nice." Roland shook his head.

"Well, what've you got? You're not offering any ideas." Peter looked Roland over slowly. "You called us together.

You must have something. What's the deal?"

"Maybe the artist *is* sad," Kiara said, sounding sad herself. "Have we hurt someone's feelings?"

"If we're Dorian Gray," Keefe said, "we should be thinking of our faults."

"Back to confession, then, huh?" Peter smirked.

"Is Father coming tonight?" Keefe glanced at the door.

"No, Father's not coming." Peter returned to his seat on the arm of the chair. "This meeting is for us. We've got to figure this out. So, taking Keefe's idea, if we do any self-evaluation, we do it here. Together. Who wants to go first?"

Roland's gaze shot to the floor. Keefe checked his phone. And Dominic looked at the girls.

Phoebe huffed.

Kiara and Caitlyn looked at each other. Kiara's wide-eyed look said she wasn't going first, so Caitlyn scooted forward, to the edge of the couch. "Okay, I will. What am I supposed to say? Something bad about myself?"

"Say whatever you want." Peter slid into the chair and draped a leg over the arm.

Caitlyn took a breath, gathering her thoughts. "Well, everyone knows I come from a big family and we live in a little three-bedroom ranch. I love my siblings, but we do argue and fight over things, like the bathroom and the last piece of cake. And sometimes I argue with Mom, and I can be kind of mean when I argue."

"But . . ." Phoebe leaned past Kiara to peer at Caitlyn.

"No 'but.' I love my family. I mean the chaos at home

sometimes drives me crazy. But I also love it. It's just . . . when I want to have friends over, it can be sort of . . ." Her gaze slid to Roland by accident. She remembered the day he and Peter had come over. She was babysitting and couldn't go anywhere. Too embarrassed to invite them inside their messy house, she talked with them on the front porch. Unfortunately, she had food in her hair and didn't find it until later. "Well, it's always a disaster. I guess I wish we had a bigger house."

"Don't you have any real woes?" Phoebe sneered.

"Sorry." Caitlyn scooted back and smoothed her skirt. What else could she say? Her life wasn't perfect, but she liked it. And, no, she didn't have any real woes. Her family got along for the most part. No deaths. No divorce. No major illnesses. No big problems. "I guess I'll just shut up."

"You don't have to shut up." Kiara rubbed Caitlyn's shoulder. "You don't need to have major problems to share your story. Your story is important too. I mean, we all experience joys and trials and sorrows. You're just as relevant as anyone else here."

Caitlyn smiled, appreciating her sweet, considerate friend. Kiara cared about everyone.

"Okay, so what about you?" Phoebe said.

"Me?" Kiara spun to Phoebe. "Oh, I—I guess I could go next." She clasped her hands on her lap. With shy glances around the room, she shared the struggle she faced at home, how her mother was Catholic but her father wasn't and how they often argued about the faith. She'd once told

Caitlyn how sometimes their arguments got so heated Kiara worried they might separate, or worse—divorce.

"I try to be the peacemaker at home," Kiara said, "and everywhere else. I want everyone to get along. But sometimes I think I do it all wrong. I don't want to make anyone sad or to hurt anyone's feelings, so I don't always say the things I should." She stared at her hands and sighed, remorse coloring her expression. "I make compromises in my mind, and then I don't speak up when it's hard."

Caitlyn shifted in her seat. She did that sometimes too.

Phoebe squeezed Kiara's hand and smiled until Kiara looked at her. They hugged, Kiara sniffling and Caitlyn's eyes tearing at Phoebe's uncharacteristic display of sisterly love.

Then Phoebe folded her arms and looked at the ceiling, her hard demeanor returning. She went next, admitting that she spoke too much and didn't listen enough, that she'd been hard on people: her friends, her teachers, herself. She didn't like how people labeled her, or anyone else. And how some people spread rumors or told absolute lies.

Eyes cold, she shifted her gaze to Dominic.

Dominic lifted his hands. "I never spread nothing about you."

Phoebe glared until he looked away. "Except for you guys, I don't get along with many kids my own age. I don't know why. Sometimes I find it easier to talk to adult friends." She closed her eyes and pressed her lips together.

"My father's mean to my mother," she blurted, then she sucked in a deep breath.

Everyone sat in silence, all eyes filled with compassion and locked on Phoebe as she poured out the details of her rough home life. Her mother never fought back. It bothered Phoebe, but she didn't blame her because she didn't know what her mom had gone through in the past.

Her eyes narrowed as she looked toward the guys on the couch. "I will never be in that situation. I will always speak up, defend myself, fight back. And I'm not getting married until I'm absolutely sure about the guy."

Her heart breaking for Phoebe, Caitlyn barely breathed. How had she never realized any of this before? She'd never considered why Phoebe acted the way she did or what she went through at home.

"I'm sorry," Keefe whispered, saying what Caitlyn wished she'd said.

Phoebe exhaled. "So what's your story?"

She probably didn't know what to believe about the West brothers. They showed up at River Run High last year, and rumors followed. Ridiculous rumors. Cruel rumors.

Caitlyn's eyes teared again as her conscience reminded her that she'd inadvertently been responsible for gossiping about them. They'd lost their mother years ago and kids made up bizarre explanations for what had happened to her. Caitlyn had only meant to set the record straight when she'd blurted out what Roland had confided to her, that Mrs. West was dead. Unfortunately, Roland had heard her too.

Running a hand through his short brown hair, Keefe took a moment to respond. "Rumors don't bother me. Though sometimes I'd rather go through life unnoticed." His gaze slid to Roland, who seemed to prefer solitude and anonymity more than anyone Caitlyn knew. "But I don't care what people think of me. I care what God thinks of me."

"Here, here," Dominic said. "*Entendido*. If God is for us, who can be against us?"

"But I do care what people think of my brothers." Keefe stared ahead, but everyone else looked at Dominic. Keefe's twin brother, a wild sort, had a bad reputation.

Maybe it wasn't all true.

"I get the feeling you've been keeping something from us, *vato*," Dominic said. "And I am not asking so I can gossip about it. You've just been quieter than usual. You've got something going on, no?"

Keefe opened and then closed his mouth, color sliding up his neck.

"Drop it, Dominic." Slouching in the armchair, Peter waved a hand at him. "It's your turn to talk. What do you have to confess and who are your enemies?" He waved his hand again, faster. "Nah, forget your enemies. We don't have time for that list."

Dominic laughed. Then he shared how, coming from a big, close-knit family with many traditions, he was Catholic by default. "Not that I don't love my religion. I do. But I take it for granted, maybe don't live it as deeply as I should. I need to change a few things."

Pausing, he shifted in his seat and his expression turned thoughtful. "It would not have surprised me if I had been the only one in the painting, the way I've handled things in my life." Then he reminded everyone of how God had touched his life by healing him, a miracle they'd all witnessed last year. He realized, too, that he didn't respond to the grace as well as he should've. He knew that God wanted him to change some things in his life. "I'm sure you all know what I'm talking about. I'm kind of a gossip."

Smiles and restrained giggles went around the room.

"Some things are none of my business. I don't know why I do it. I guess I like the way people come to me with things." He shook his head the way he used to before the haircut, when his hair hung in his eyes. "I like to feel important. If I don't have that, what do I have?"

"You've got us, man." Peter tugged a throw-pillow from behind him and tossed it at Dominic. "We know you can't help it."

"He can help it," Phoebe said, folding her arms.

"Well, it sounds like he wants to change," Kiara the peace-maker said. "That's half the battle, right? None of us is perfect. We all have something to overcome."

Caitlyn never once considered that Dominic recognized he had a problem, or the reasons why he gossiped, or that he wanted to change.

"Speaking of which . . ." Peter looked at Roland. "You're next, Roland."

Roland jerked back, panic in his eyes. "I don't have anything to say. What are we accomplishing by this, anyway?"

"You must have something to say. Everyone else said something." Peter waved a hand.

"You didn't."

Peter laughed. "Okay, so I'll go next." He got up, glancing from face to face. "You've all shared some really personal things." He stopped by Roland and kicked his boot. "Except for you. So I can try to dig deep, too."

Peter paced the floor, eyes on the painting when he faced that direction. "Who am I? What are my faults? What could anyone have against me?" He lifted a hand. "I like my games, my entertainment. And I have things I like to do—make gadgets and repair stuff—and I'm maybe a bit self-involved. I think I could be perfectly happy by myself. Not that I don't like all of you." He made a sweeping gesture to indicate them.

The group responded with a few sarcastic comments.

"And I don't consider myself a loner." Peter toed Roland's boot again, Roland rolling his eyes. "But wouldn't it be nice? No one to make me load the dishwasher and cut the grass, no one to tell me to watch my younger brother or to do schoolwork. But . . . I'm coming to see that I need people. My family. My friends. Maybe that's a given to all of you, but I'm gradually starting to get it. God put all these people in my life, and some of them even need me. Like this one here who doesn't like to speak." He stood before Roland.

Roland shook his head and gave a threatening look.

"So let me tell you about Roland."

"No you don't." Roland jumped up and stood close to Peter.

Peter grinned and shoved Roland back. "Roland came to River Run High last year and didn't know anybody. Didn't have any friends, a bit of a loner. But now we're like best friends. Right?"

Roland shook his head, his face turning crimson. "Not sure."

"I think he could've had a lot more friends, even in the beginning, but he had a hard time trusting and feeling accepted."

"Talk about yourself."

"I'm getting there."

"Get there faster." Roland shoved Peter.

Grinning, Peter shoved back. "So, what makes a person feel left out?"

"You're not talking about me, right?" Body rigid, Roland pushed into Peter's space.

A strange guttural noise made Caitlyn turn her head. The janitor rushed into the room and squeezed between Roland and Peter, the three of them stumbling over each other's feet. He shook his head and signed something, slicing the air, then crossing his arms, his hands fisted. He sliced the air again.

"It's okay, buddy." Peter touched his shoulder. "We're just messing around."

Roland returned to the couch and flopped down.

The janitor nodded and backed up. He looked at Roland one last time and shuffled from the room.

"Okay, I was trying to make a point. God puts people in our lives, in our families and our circles, because we need each other. But we don't always appreciate that." Peter gestured widely as he spoke.

Peter had Caitlyn's attention. Now, typically, whenever he spoke, he said something funny, sarcastic, or annoying. But this time, she agreed with him. And after hearing everyone share their problems, determination rose within her. She was going to be a better friend to every one of them. Each one was in her life for a reason!

"Like my younger brother, Toby," Peter continued. "He's got autism and can be quite a pest, but I know he needs my attention. And I need him. He makes me more patient, caring, and humbled. I know it makes Toby sad when I don't have time for him. He doesn't feel like he's important to me. Maybe he even knows he's different, and he wishes he wasn't. Maybe he feels that his differences —"

Peter stepped back, stumbling on something. "—make him less . . ." He dropped his gaze to the floor, and his face drained of color. ". . . less important."

Moving in slow motion, he lifted his head and turned it to the door. Then he opened his mouth. A moment later, he spoke. "His differences make him feel like he's less important. He's about our age, and we don't give him the time of day."

"What?" Phoebe said.

"Is he still talking about Toby?" Kiara said.

"Guys," Peter said. "I think I know who our artist is. And I think I know what the painting means." He stooped and picked up something from the floor.

Caitlyn gasped. A paintbrush? The janitor must've dropped it when he'd tried to break up their fight.

Her skin prickled and her conscience stirred as she turned to the door. Realization dawned on her. All this time . . . She'd seen him every time she came up for the Fire Starters meetings. He'd even tried communicating with her, hadn't he? And he could've been about their age. Regardless . . . God put him in their life. How could she have been so thoughtless?

"Oh, man," Keefe said.

Roland and Peter stood face to face again, sharing repentant expressions.

"Wow, we messed up," Phoebe said. Kiara nodded.

"I guess we won't be leaving the room in such a mess anymore," Dominic said. "And maybe we should invite him—"

Could we all learn sign language? Caitlyn wondered. *Of course we could!*

But for now . . . Eyes welling with tears, Caitlyn ran from the room to find him.

The characters in this short story are also in the *West Brothers* series. The *West Brothers* series is contemporary Catholic teen fiction about three teenage brothers who

live in a castle-like house, complete with battlements and a secret passage. In the first book, they are new to River Run High School. This is a problem for Roland, who is incredibly shy. But it's not a problem at all for his older twin brothers, who exude confidence. The three brothers don't always know the right thing to do but they grow and change over the years, finding answers to life's questions in the treasure of the Faith. Two books in this series won awards from the Catholic Press Association, but Theresa Linden's favorite "award" comes from reluctant readers who can relate to the characters, love the books, and encourage her to write more in this series.

ABOUT THE AUTHOR

THERESA LINDEN is the author of the *Chasing Liberty* dystopian trilogy and the *West Brothers* series, including Catholic Press Association award-winners *Roland West, Loner* and *Battle for His Soul.* She resides in Ohio with her husband and their three teen sons. A Secular Franciscan and a member of the Catholic Writers Guild, her faith inspires the belief that there is no greater adventure than the realities we can't see, the spiritual side of life. She hopes that her stories will spark her readers' imaginations and awaken them to the power of faith and grace. Learn more about her and find her social media links at www.TheresaLinden.com.

4

ON THE BRINK OF HELL

by Susan Peek

16th Century Italy

White-hot pain exploded through Dario with every bounce and jolt of the makeshift stretcher. Try as he might, he couldn't stop tears of agony from sliding down his cheeks as the four soldiers jogged along as fast as they dared with their awkward burden. They shoved their way through the crowd, swerving his stretcher around horses and wagons and noisy market stalls, cursing and jostling people aside as they ran.

"Move! Move! Out of our way!"

A woman in a dyed green cloak carrying a basket got stuck in their path. She veered one way then the other, not knowing which way to go. When she saw Dario, she recoiled, aghast, and her basket crashed to the ground. Fruit spilled into the rutted street, nearly tripping up the soldiers. The stretcher tipped dangerously.

The woman grabbed the little girl beside her, trying to jerk her back. She wasn't quick enough.

"His legs! Mama! Oh my gosh, oh my gosh! That man's legs are missing!"

"Sweetheart, don't look! Don't—"

"Out of the way! Move it, move it!"

Dario's chest constricted with fear as his comrades righted the stretcher and flew past the horror-stricken pair. Were . . . were his legs . . . *gone*? Terror bolted through him. There had been so much blood when they hauled him off the battlefield and bundled him into the cart. Blood had run everywhere, saturating his clothes, soaking the planks beneath him. He'd assumed it was from the deep gashes in his chest and stomach. Now he realized with horror why the soldiers kept pushing him down every time he'd tried to sit up during the ride into Rome. Had the cannonball blown off his legs? *Dear God, no. Please no.* He squeezed his eyes shut, fighting panic. *Both legs?* Bile rose in his throat. He was going to be sick.

"I keep telling you, he's not gonna make it," one of the soldiers said above the stretcher, as if Dario couldn't hear him. Maybe they thought he'd lost consciousness. He kept slipping in and out.

"Orders are orders. The commander said to get him to a hospital."

The stretcher bounced up and down, Dario's stomach with it.

"Which commander?"

"That young one. Recently promoted. Can't think of his

name."

"Antoni?"

"Yep, sounds right. Apparently they're friends."

Another soldier said, "Where's the blasted hospital?"

"Should be close."

"I see it! That's San Giacomo, there on the left."

The stretcher lurched wildly as the four soldiers broke into a run. Every motion jarred Dario with a fresh blast of torture.

Then, thank God, darkness finally swallowed him again.

"Shh. Just lie still. He's nearly done." A male voice, hushed and comforting, nudged its way through the blackness and pain.

Dario stirred, the motion triggering waves of agony. His head felt like mortar had been poured into it. Where was he? Who was nearly done . . . and with what?

A hand squeezed his, warmth and compassion radiating from the stranger's grip. As if reading his mind, the man whispered, "It's alright. You're in a hospital."

Why was he whispering?

Dario was about to open his eyes, when someone— presumably the *he* who was almost done with *something*— prevented him by lightly touching his eyelids. Dario sucked in a breath, heart hammering. What was the person going to do? Was this an operation? An involuntary whimper escaped him as he braced himself for whatever torture was to come. The one holding his hand tightened his grip.

Dario waited, breathless, his eyelids still held down.

Seconds ticked by. He lay frozen, unable to breathe, imagining all the nightmare procedures done on soldiers after battle. He'd seen them all. In fact, he'd even performed a few over the years to save comrades on the field.

Quietly spoken words, foreign and incomprehensible, floated above the bed.

Nothing else happened. No knife. No flaming alcohol poured into his wounds. No red-hot iron pressed into his flesh to cauterize an open gash. No thick needle stitching his shredded, broken body together.

Why was nothing happening?

Disturbing noises from elsewhere in the room assaulted his ears, prickling his skin with goosebumps. Someone was screaming in pain, someone else crying. More than one voice begged loudly for water, only to be answered with swearing. The hand around Dario's tightened, like a silent plea to ignore it. Dario tried to block the hellish sounds, his fear escalating. Maybe it was a good thing his eyes were being held shut after all.

"It's alright." The one squeezing his hand tried to assure him for the second time.

Really? Dario didn't think so.

He forced himself to breathe, concentrating with all his might on the foreign words being recited above him, trying to ignore the heartrending noises of the ward. The words' rhythm and flow sounded oddly familiar, and something unexpected stirred in his heart. The chaos in the background seemed to fade as a gentle peace enveloped Dario's soul. For a split-second he almost forgot his searing pain.

The fingertips moved from his eyelids to his ears. Then to his nose. There was a faint scent, somehow reminding him of the olive groves back home. More strange utterances. Why did Dario recognize the words? They weren't Italian. They were . . . something else. He knew them from somewhere in his past. Where? What language was this?

He kept his eyes closed, unwilling to look at the source of the noises around him. The fingers found his mouth, brushing his lips with something moist. Instinctively Dario licked it. It was slippery. He recognized the taste. Olive oil. Why would anyone put oil on his—

Understanding slammed into him with a tidal wave of fear. He was being anointed! This must be a priest, administering Extreme Unction. That meant he was going to die!

Terror rushed upon him and instantly he knew why he recognized the language. It was Latin. The language of the Church. The Church he'd grown up in. And later betrayed.

He suddenly knew what would be next. His hands. Memories flooded him. As a child he'd seen his father anointed. His aunt. Both grandparents. Folks in the village, when the parish priest had knocked on their door, sometimes in the middle of the night, asking Dario or one of his brothers to act as server and carry the candle and holy water. Eyes were always the first things the priest anointed, followed by ears, nose, mouth. Hands and feet last. The five senses. The faculties by which people sinned, the village priest had explained. And, without exception, all those people had died. The Church didn't do this unless the person was on the brink of death.

He didn't want to die!

Panic pulsed through Dario and he yanked his hand free from whoever was holding it. No, no, he wouldn't allow the priest to anoint his hands. He would refuse! The Church had no right to issue him a death warrant. For that's what this ceremony was—a proclamation that he, Dario Tellini, was about to die. How dare they decide that! He wouldn't let them. He would never give in! He tried to sit up, anger surging.

Pain spiked like a million swords ramming through his body and he collapsed back to the pillow. A moan escaped him. The man beside him, the one speaking in ordinary language, murmured soothing words.

The priest anointed his hands.

Dario groaned, his anger draining as that consoling *something* fluttered in his soul again. His feet would be next. He might as well give in and—

The ritual stopped abruptly. A crinkling of pages, then a muffled thump as a book was gently closed.

The priest and the other man exchanged whispered words that Dario couldn't make out. Suddenly a door banged open, interrupting them. Loud urgent voices and cacophony erupted somewhere in the room.

Dario sensed quick movements by his bed. Footsteps hurrying away. The priest? The other man? Which one was leaving?

His eyes darted open.

A young man was sitting beside him. He looked to be in his early twenties, like Dario, but his expression shone with something Dario had not seen in a long, long time: innocence. It was so startling that for a moment Dario stared. The fellow wore a blood-splattered tunic and trousers. Definitely not the priest. Must be a hospital worker. An orderly.

Dario's mind whirled. Why had the priest not finished administering Extreme Unction? He hadn't anointed Dario's feet yet. That always came after the hands. Dario knew. He'd seen it as a child.

The memory blasted him like an icy gale. He had no feet. His legs were gone.

Nausea churned his stomach. He was going to throw up. The orderly must have realized, because he fumbled for a pan. The next second Dario was leaning on the fellow's shoulder, half-sitting, doubled over, being violently sick.

The other held the pan for him, without the least sign of annoyance or revulsion. In fact, the kindness of his manner was tangible. When the ordeal was over, he helped Dario lie back down and tried his best to make him comfortable—as if that held any possibility with his legs laying somewhere in a field.

An elderly man shuffled by the bed. He was a thousand

years old. In his gnarled hands he held a pile of bloodied sheets. His tunic was likewise splotched with blood and hospital filth of a species that Dario preferred not to know.

The fossil glanced at Dario and stopped, eyes misting. "Hang in there, brave fellow." He blinked back what Dario suspected were tears. "Them good angels will wing you to your reward soon, my boy, don't you worry." As if that was what Dario wanted to hear. The wrinkled face turned to the young orderly. "I'll get these to the laundry, then I'll take over here. You've done three shifts today, Curzio. You need some sleep."

Was he also an orderly? At that age? He looked for all the world like he belonged in a hospital bed himself.

"Thanks, Bernadino," the one named Curzio said. "But I'm good. I'll stay with him."

Bernadino hesitated. "Well, I'll be back." The two exchanged the kind of look that only the closest of friends could share, then the old man limped away with the sheets.

Dario watched him for a moment, trying to fight down rising fear. He had no legs. He was gashed open by sword blades, riddled by musket bullets, ripped in half by a cannonball. He was dying. He had never been more afraid in his life. Uncontrollable trembling took over his body.

Curzio reached down and brushed the sweat-drenched hair from Dario's forehead as if he were a child. "I'll get you some laudanum. It'll help the pain."

While he moved to a nearby table, Dario dared to glance around. The room was crammed with beds. People moaned. Some rocked back and forth, sobbing. The lucky ones looked like they were in comas. A handful of orderlies moved between patients with trays and bottles of medicine. Unlike Curzio and Bernadino, most appeared sullen, angry, or bored out of their wits.

Dario swallowed. The soldiers who'd brought him here had left. The priest who'd anointed him was nowhere in sight. The stench of blood and decay was suffocating. Chaos reigned in the ward. Dear God, this place was more frightening than a battlefield. Were all hospitals like this? If so, why didn't someone do anything about it?

The instant the thought came, Dario realized the impossibility of reforming a place like this. It would take a person of iron will, extraordinary courage, and incredible devotion. In other words, it would take a saint. *Good luck, Rome.*

His gaze searched in desperation for someone, anyone, who looked like he might be a doctor, might be in charge. Everyone was too young, except Bernadino. Not one person struck Dario as a figure of authority. From the expression on most of the workers' faces, they had little compassion for their charges. They stalked moodily from bed to bed, obviously hardened to the sufferings around them. Dario shuddered.

"Here. This tastes awful, but it'll dull the pain a little. And help you sleep."

Dario's eyes fluttered to Curzio by the bed. Well, at least he seemed to care. Dario was lucky. He let Curzio lift his head and spoon a few drops of bitter liquid into his mouth. Then Curzio put a cup of water to his lips to wash it down. After Dario drank, Curzio rearranged the sheet over the bandaged blood-drenched stumps that had once been his legs, as if to keep Dario from having to see his loss.

"I'm going to find you more blankets," Curzio said. "You're shivering."

Dario didn't want to be left alone. He tried to protest, but before he could get his mouth to work, Curzio disappeared into the crowded ward.

Dario pushed back panic. Would a doctor come and assure him his legs could be reattached, his other wounds weren't fatal, and everything would be fine? *Please God, please please please.*

But deep in his heart he knew no doctor would bother. That soldier had been right—Dario would never make it. He was finished. He was nothing but a breathing cadaver on a creaky bed for an hour or two, after which he'd be wrapped up by one of these bored orderlies, wheeled away on a gurney, and dumped into some unmarked grave. Just another dead, nameless soldier. And a mercenary soldier at that. Who bothered marking the grave of a hireling?

Hireling. Ha! That was too gentle a word. Most people would call Dario a traitor, a greedy swordsman who fought for whichever side paid him the most. A Judas. An enemy of Christendom. A betrayer of Christ.

And they would be right.

Panic, mingled with guilt, stabbed him. He realized he

should have asked the priest to hear his confession. He'd once fought on the side of the Turks. Sure, it had only been for a couple months, but he'd still done it. Was . . . was he in mortal sin? Or had the priest's anointing erased that evil blotch from his soul?

Dear God, what if I go to Hell for wielding my sword against Christendom?

Fear swelled in his chest. He was going to Hell.

Inch by agonizing inch, he propped himself on one elbow. Pain ricocheted through him. Biting back a cry, he desperately looked around. He needed that priest to come back! He had to make his confession, before that drug put him to sleep!

An orderly stood at a bed a few feet away, savagely ripping a bandage off some poor fellow's arm. The man was sobbing.

A bead of sweat dripped down Dario's forehead. "Help me," he begged.

The orderly glanced up. "Huh?"

"That priest . . ." Pain wracked Dario's lungs and scorched his throat, making it hard to speak. "I need . . ."

The orderly rolled his eyes, a smirk twisting his mouth. "He left for the night."

"Please. You don't understand. You need to bring him back."

The worker glared. "I don't need to do anything for you, legless. What are you, deaf, too? I said the priest left. Won't be back until morning. Now shut up and leave me to do my work."

Too weak to stay propped up, Dario collapsed on the bed. Such a comment would normally unleash his fury, ensuring those were the last words the man ever said. But all Dario felt now was despair.

He'd fought for the Turks. The enemy. He'd crucified the Lord he'd once claimed to love. His soul was in mortal sin.

And the priest had left!

A memory knifed him, and he winced. It was a venomous memory, cruel with irony. Why did he have to think of it now? He cringed and squeezed his eyes shut, as if that would make the memory disappear.

It didn't.

In fact, the remembrance grew more vivid.

The tavern of the inn was empty, except for the two of them.

Not surprising, considering the snow storm raging outside. That was good. Maybe not for Signor Vitali, the innkeeper, but certainly for Dario and Antoni. It left them all the wine.

Dario knew he should call it a day and get some rest. They'd traveled a long way and had an even longer way to go to meet the troops in Venice. But the crackling fire kept Dario warm. So did the contents of his cup. Besides, Antoni was winning the card game, and that was totally unacceptable. Dario would have none of it.

"You're cheating," he said, although he knew Antoni wasn't. Antoni couldn't figure out how to cheat to save his life.

Antoni cocked an eyebrow and grinned in that irresistible way of his. "Ever heard of beginner's luck?"

"Doesn't apply. You're not a beginner. You've been losing since the moment I met you. Must be . . . what? Two years? Three?"

"Hmm. You're right. Guess I don't qualify for beginner's luck." Antoni studied the cards in his hand and frowned, as if trying to unravel an unsolvable mystery. Then his face brightened. "Hey, maybe it's skill!" He wiggled his eyebrows and looked appealingly at Dario. "Think it's skill?"

"Skill? You?" Dario laughed. "Has Hell frozen over?"

The door crashed open and a blast of icy wind shoved two men inside. Dario glanced over. Talk about Hell. He didn't know it at the time, but his own journey thither started with the entrance of those two snow-dusted strangers.

The muskets and swords at their sides proclaimed they were soldiers, like he and Antoni. Dario was taken aback by the size of one of them. The man barely fit through Signor Vitali's door. Young—about his own age and Antoni's—the fellow must've been nearly seven feet tall. The first thing Dario noticed about him, other than his size, was the arrogant glint in his eyes. Big, muscular, and showing it off. For some reason, instant antipathy stirred inside Dario.

The other soldier was middle-aged and, despite his normal stature, looked strong as an ox and mean as a bull. But right now, he was breathing hard, as if trekking through the blizzard had taken its toll.

Father and son? Had to be.

They swaggered inside and fought the door closed behind them. Pride seeped from them like slime.

Amazingly, Signor Vitali cracked a smile and wiped his

hands on his apron, rushing to the door. He offered the older man a handshake and laughed. "Well, if it isn't Giovanni de Lellis and his wayward offspring."

Yep. Father and son. Dario knew it.

Antoni must have recognized the name, because he swiveled in his chair to look. "Oh no!" he called out. "Why is it that whenever I'm on one of my rare winning streaks, you two always show up and spoil it?"

Antoni knew them? Huh. Strange. Even stranger, he was grinning, as if they were old friends.

The giant stamped the snow from his boots and strode to their table. He had a limp. "Seriously, Antoni, you didn't think you could get away with a card game without us smelling it halfway across the border, did you?" He punched Antoni's shoulder.

Antoni shook his head and heaved a sigh. But a smile sneaked through. "Should've known better. Happens every time." He turned to Dario. "You don't want to meet this fellow in a card game, Dario."

Dario didn't want to meet him—at all. Something about him raised Dario's hackles. He couldn't explain why, but he sensed this fellow was bad news. Dangerous. Looking for a fight.

Antoni sprang to his feet. "Guess I better do the polite thing and introduce you two. Dario Tellini . . . Camillus de Lellis." His voice held affection for both.

Dario dutifully stood and shook hands. Camillus didn't say anything, just sized Dario up. Maybe it had something to do with the card game. Or perhaps the instinctive dislike was mutual. Dario had heard of things like that. Two people meet, the chemistry is bad, and bang, you have an enemy for no logical reason.

"Haven't seen you and your old man for ages." Antoni sat down. "Where've you been?"

Camillus shrugged and pulled up a chair. "Soldiering as usual." He plopped down. Hesitation flickered in his eyes for the briefest of moments. He shifted uncomfortably and mumbled, "Only this time . . . well . . . we've just been doing it for the other side, that's all."

Antoni jolted in shock. He cocked an eyebrow, yet held his peace. Dario suspected he was biting his tongue.

As for Dario, a wave of rage washed over him. He glared at the mercenary with disgust, but before he could think of an appropriately stinging remark, the two older men sauntered over with drinks.

"So, Giovanni," Signor Vitali was saying, "what high and mighty commander was it this time who could no longer bear you two scoundrels in his ranks?"

Camillus's father chuckled. "Would you believe it? The Sultan himself." Amusement glinted in his beady eyes. "Heathenish Turk can't recognize a couple decent soldiers when they're staring him in the face."

Dario's blood boiled. "Decent?" he sneered, before he could stop himself.

The older De Lellis looked startled, as if unaccustomed to being crossed. He met Dario's gaze.

Everything inside Dario warned him to shut up. But the bold words slipped out before he could weigh the consequences. "No Christian soldier is decent, Signor de Lellis, who is willing to take up arms with the Infidel against God and His people."

An icy silence dropped into the room. Everyone froze.

Dario's heart thumped wildly. Why had he thrown down the gauntlet like that? Stupid move. His hand tingled as he wondered whether or not he would need to go for his sword.

No need. Giovanni de Lellis merely rolled his eyes, snorted a laugh, and poured himself a drink. Apparently, Dario wasn't worth his time.

His son, however, took up the challenge. He locked eyes with Dario.

Danger hung heavily in the air.

"God and His people didn't pay us enough." Camillus smirked. "The Turks did."

Dario tensed.

Camillus had found his fight.

Dario swallowed, forcing the uncomfortable memory away. Thankfully, no blood had been shed between them. At least not that time. That came later. Antoni, as usual, had defused the situation. Some lighthearted joke, a slap on the back, a pacifying goblet shoved into Camillus's hands.

What raked Dario's conscience on his deathbed was his own sickening self-righteousness. Who would've believed that he, who'd posed as such an outstanding Catholic, would someday commit the same treachery himself? Yep, times had gotten hard and money had run out. In desperation Dario had hired his blade to the same Sultan served by De Lellis and his son. In the end, Dario turned as wicked as they. Even more, for his hypocrisy.

And he would pay the price. By tomorrow morning, at the latest, he'd be burning in the fires of Hell. A shudder ran through him. Fear clamped his lungs.

"Look at you shiver, boy. I'll try to rustle up a blanket."

Huh? Dario opened his eyes. Bernadino leaned over him, his ancient face creased with worry.

"I move slower'n a snail, but if you'll be patient, I'll fetch a—"

"I already brought some." Curzio appeared at the foot of the bed and dumped an armload of blankets where Dario's legs should be. "Are you feeling sleepy yet? That laudanum should kick in soon."

Dario nodded, drowsiness overcoming him.

Curzio tucked the blankets around his shivering torso. He must've spotted the fear in Dario's eyes because he stopped and said, "Are you alright? Would it help to talk?"

Bernadino leaned in. "We're here for you, son. We're here."

Dario's eyes misted. These two strangers really cared. Yet . . . what could he say to them? How could he unburden his sins to anyone but a priest? How would these two even understand his terror of Hell? Curzio looked pure as an angel. And Bernadino may have strayed from the straight-and-narrow in his past, but probably not in ninety years.

No, Dario couldn't tell them he was damned, couldn't let them know the abhorrence of what he'd done. If they knew he'd sided with the enemy, even briefly, they'd . . .

they'd be repulsed. They'd walk away. Leave him to die alone.

"We're here, lad." Bernadino laid a skeletal hand on Dario's arm.

Dario ached to confide in them, to pour out his contrition. But they would never relate to his fear. Only another soldier could. Another mercenary who'd known hunger and temptation and despair and had crucified Christ to fill his belly. A soldier would understand. But not these two.

Dario shook his head and closed his eyes, burying himself in agonized silence. If only it had been merely siding with the enemy for a few weeks. Then perhaps God could forgive him that one terrible crime. But no, Dario had offended his gentle Savior more than once. Even before he'd hired himself to the Turks, there had been that first mortal sin. A great big whopping mortal sin. The night he'd gotten drunk.

"Oh no," Dario groaned the instant he saw Camillus seated at the outside table. What was he doing here? Over a thousand men in this army, and they'd have to invite the one soldier who grated Dario's nerves raw. Ending up together in the same troop had been bad enough, but finding Camillus dealing the cards was beyond endurance. Someone should have known not to allow Camillus here when Dario was planning to play. Antoni should have been onto it. Or Jacopo, or Ty.

Wait, no. Forget Ty. He was already plastered beyond plastered, and the evening had hardly begun. Couldn't even locate the deck of cards on the table in front of him, let alone recognize the players. All Ty could focus on, as usual, was the cup in his hand. He was doing an outstanding job just remaining propped in a chair without toppling into the campfire.

But the others. They weren't all drunk. Not yet anyhow. Close, yessss—Dario included—but surely at least Antoni knew how Dario felt about Camillus. So why'd they invite the rat to join them in the first place?

Somehow, he'd managed to ignore Camillus for the first hour or two of cards. Now they were at the eighth hand. Or . . . was it the eighth game? Dario frowned at his cards, trying to remember. His head was getting fuzzy. Maybe it was the eighth cask of wine he was thinking of. Things were colliding together in his brain at the moment. But one thing he knew with crystal clarity: Camillus, that swine, had won every round.

Every.

Single.

Round.

All night long.

And there was only one humanly possible way to do that.

Camillus took a swig from his tankard, tossed everyone a sickening smile, then chucked his cards face up on the table. Everyone groaned. Another perfect win.

Maybe it was the wine, maybe it was all the money Dario had lost, or maybe it was just that burning grudge, but something inside him snapped. He slammed his fist on the table so hard the planks jumped. He pierced Camillus with a look spilling straight from the hatred in his heart.

"Alright, De Lellis. Enough is enough. What's your game?"

Camillus barely spared him a glance. Sweeping the pile of money towards himself, he didn't deign to reply. He calmly took another sip of his drink.

Dario exploded. "You've won every hand we've played. Are the extras up your sleeve or down your boot?"

Camillus looked up. His face darkened.

An uncomfortable hush fell around the table. Worried glances flew left and right. Dario's muscles tensed, but he wasn't going to back down. Camillus was cheating, and it was as obvious as the nose on his face.

All the players seemed to hold their breath. Everyone except Ty, who was scrutinizing a lone card in his hand as if it had dropped from the moon. By the bewildered expression on his face, he had no idea what the thing was or how it'd materialized in his grip.

Camillus clenched one of his giant fists. His jaw twitched as he visibly struggled for self-control. When he finally spoke, his voice was low, and quiet . . . and oh so deadly.

"Take that back, Tellini."

Dario felt, rather than saw, the pleading eyes of his comrades boring into him. They were silently begging him to retract his accusation. Antoni cleared his throat, doubtless about to intervene, when Camillus gave Dario a second chance.

"I said: Take. That. Back."

Dario should. Not because he changed his mind about Camillus cheating, but because Camillus was nearly seven feet tall with muscles of concrete. Never mind that he walked with a severe limp from some old wound. He was still a giant. And not just any ol' giant, but a drunken one. He could crush Dario's skull with his bare hands. Dario didn't even have his sword. If anything happened, it would be a hand-to-hand fight.

The instinct for survival should have pounced into action. But right now, compliments of those eight empty casks, Dario was just as drunk as Camillus. Life versus death didn't cross his mind. The only thing that crossed it was how much he despised Camillus de-Spicable Lellis.

Laughter rose in Dario's throat. Laughter spawned from hatred. "Take it back? Take it back from the crippled son of a traitorous pig father?"

Camillus rocketed from his chair, rather like a cannonball launching. "What?!"

"You heard me, you useless crip—"

The table up-ended, slamming straight into Dario's face with the force of a battering ram. He crashed to the ground, his head exploding in pain, the table smashing on top of him. Wine splashed onto his lap, cups and coins slid, and cards fluttered everywhere.

Dazed, Dario tried to scramble from the wreckage. He wasn't quick enough. The giant heaved the table aside and landed on top of him. Fists pummeled his face. Bones cracked. Blood spurted. Shouts deafened his ears.

"Take it easy, Camillus!"

"Let him go! You'll kill him!"

Soldiers were grabbing Camillus, yelling and swearing.

It took three of them to haul the brute off. But that wasn't the end of it. The following morning came Dario's next mortal sin.

He and Camillus fought a duel.

He flinched at the memory, and realized he was clutching the blankets tightly in his fists. Bernadino wrung out a cloth and dabbed it to his forehead, stroking Dario's hair with his paper-thin hands. Suddenly Dario wanted him and Curzio to leave. They shouldn't be near him. These two orderlies were too good, too pure, to be tending a demon.

Getting drunk was bad enough. But what would Curzio and Bernadino think if they knew he'd fought a duel the next morning? Dueling was a mortal sin, forbidden by the Church. And Dario couldn't even blame the wine anymore. When he unsheathed his sword against Camillus, he'd been stone cold sober.

And had full intent to kill.

The two blades clashed and clanged with ferocious violence and frightening speed. Dario might not be a match for Camillus in hand-to-hand combat, but he could hold his own with a sword. In fact, after the first few slashes, Camillus's cockiness withered and vanished, and a look of worry sparked in his eyes. Seeing his growing fear bloated Dario with delight.

Parry. Fade. Parry again.

Pass forward.

Sidestep. Feint and . . . Lunge!

Yes! Dario's blade ripped across Camillus's shoulder and a jagged red line seeped through his sleeve. Staggering, Camillus almost went down and fumbled to keep his sword.

Dario slashed again, victory welling, feeding his lust for Camillus's blood.

The group of soldiers surrounding them yelled, cheered, swore.

Camillus retreated a few paces, then regained his footing and passed forward. He lashed out. A bolt of pain tore Dario's face, followed by a warm rush of blood. Fury filled him. He flew at Camillus, hating him, wanting nothing but to rip his heart out and send him to Hell.

Another sickening jolt of metal sliced his flesh. Agony. Dario's vision blurred. He parried, then blindly whipped his sword through the air.

Missed.

Camillus managed a clumsy strike. With a yelp of pain, Dario lost his grip on his sword's slippery hilt. The weapon flew from his hand and thudded into the dirt a few feet away. In a heartbeat, Camillus crashed into him, slamming him to the ground, and shoved his blade to Dario's throat. Icy steel pressed against his neck.

This was it. Dario was going to die. And for what? A few coins lost in a card game.

He squeezed his eyes closed as beads of sweat dripped down his brow. Any second now Camillus would slit his throat and —

Camillus dropped the sword.

BANG! A deafening gunshot blasted the air.

Startled, Dario's eyes shot open. A few feet away a horse stamped and snorted. Upon its back sat their commanding officer. Rage blazed in his eyes. Smoke still floated from the barrel of the pistol he'd shot into the air.

Camillus scrambled to his feet.

Something niggled at Dario. Hadn't that happened in the

wrong order? The shot should have sounded first, making Camillus drop his sword. Yet he'd released Dario an instant before the pistol went off.

Had . . . had Camillus spared him willingly? He must have.

Bewildered, Dario staggered to his wobbly legs. He was alive. He should be dead, but he wasn't.

Dario sucked in a ragged breath, sleepiness overwhelming him. The laudanum must've been working. Bernadino dipped the cloth in the water again, squeezed it out, and pressed it to his forehead. Curzio changed the blood-drenched bandage on his chest, looking sad. Guess they'd given up on him talking to them.

Dario should say something. They wanted to offer him comfort in his last hours. But he couldn't bring himself to speak of his past, his fears. If he'd died the day of the duel, he would have gone straight to Hell. But God had spared him.

Camillus had spared him.

Why? Their commander hadn't stopped him from slitting Dario's throat. The officer appeared *after* Camillus tossed aside his sword. Which could only mean Camillus was unwilling to kill him. Dario couldn't fathom why. After all, Camillus was the one who'd proposed their duel in the first place. It made no sense.

Their commander had been blazing mad. Kicked Camillus out of the army, right then and there. Ty, too, for his drunkenness. Camillus had stormed away through the trees, Ty lurching after him, with nothing but their weapons, the clothes on their backs, and Ty's half-empty flask. Dario had never seen either of them again.

His eyelids drooped. His breathing slowed. The drug was taking effect.

Within seconds, sleep wrapped him in its folds.

Dario didn't know how long he'd been in that pain-filled slumber, but it must have been awhile. When he opened his eyes, the ward was dark. Most patients were quiet. Asleep. Maybe even dead. Who would care? A few candles flickered here and there in the room.

Someone squeezed his hand. "You're awake."

Curzio?

Dario slowly turned his head. No, not Curzio. The wavering candlelight revealed a stranger in the chair beside his bed. It was too dark to make out his features, but he sounded young. Dario's age perhaps. It was hard to tell, because the man's voice seemed strained, as if he were unwell and struggling to hide it. Another patient?

"The pain must be killing you. I've got laudanum right here." The man plucked a spoon and a bottle of medicine from his lap. So, not a patient. A worker. The fellow must've been waiting all along to give the drug to Dario, as if anxious to take away the agony the very moment he stirred. Dario was touched by his kindness. Still, he wished it were one of the other two. At least they were familiar faces in this terrifying place.

The man scooted his chair closer to the bed. The movement must have hurt him, because he winced. Then he measured medicine into the spoon.

"Are . . . are you a doctor?" Hope squeezed Dario's chest.

The other shook his head, and Dario's hope deflated.

"No. I'm sorry. I wish I were."

"Where's Curzio? And Bernadino?"

"I sent them to get some sleep. If I didn't order them to, they'd never quit." The man drew in a sharp breath, as if some pain had just stabbed him. "I'm the Superintendent. Curzio asked me to come down here. Now let me help you sit up so I can give you this horrible stuff."

This man was in charge of the hospital? Seriously? Dario was stunned. Not only was the fellow obviously hurt himself, but he sounded so young. Only someone incredibly trustworthy and competent could land such a high position at a young age.

The stranger carefully raised Dario's head to give him the drug. As Dario gagged down the pungent liquid, a thought struck. If this man truly was the Superintendent, he could get the priest to return and hear Dario's confession. It was the middle of the night, yes, but surely the head of the hospital could do anything.

"I need a priest. Please."

Without getting up, the Superintendent placed the bottle of medicine on the floor by his chair. "A priest already came. Curzio told me." He squeezed Dario's hand again. "You're lucky. I mean, not with your legs gone and all, but your soul. You're going straight to Heaven, Dario. God is so good."

"No, you . . . don't understand. I need to make my confession." He had to convince the Superintendent to fetch a priest! There was only one way to do that in the middle of the night. Dario cringed and strained out the words. "I . . . I'm in mortal sin." He lowered his eyes, shame burning through him. "I'm going to Hell. I . . ." He swallowed. "I once fought for the Turks."

Dead silence.

Dario didn't dare look up. Heat flared across his cheeks. Shame and remorse seared through him. The Superintendent must be staring at him, shocked. Repulsed. Who could blame the man?

The chair creaked as the other shifted. Dario winced. Was he leaving in disgust?

The Superintendent finally spoke. His words were quiet, gentle. "So did I."

Dario blinked. His gaze shot to the man, but the darkness obscured him.

"You heard me right, Dario. I hired my sword to the enemy, too. But God forgave me. His mercy is infinite. I did a lot of terrible things. Things much, much worse than you did."

How could this man have knowledge of the things Dario had done? Impossible. But the part about hiring his sword to the Turks—Dario was taken aback. "You're . . . a soldier?"

"Used to be." The Superintendent rubbed his leg. "Until *this* stopped me." He paused, then corrected himself. "No, I take that back. My crippled leg didn't stop me. God's mercy did. I should have been in Hell so many times." He sighed, as if shaking off the sadness, and his tone changed to one of hope. "But instead of being in Hell, I'm here, trying to figure out a way to fix this rotten hospital. And you're here, too, getting ready to fly to Heaven. God's mercy is staggering."

His grip tightened around Dario's hand and he leaned closer, his eyes blazing in the candlelight with an almost heavenly glow. Despite the darkness in the room, he seemed bathed in celestial light. A strange sensation pricked Dario's skin and something stirred in his heart. He knew, without a shadow of a doubt, that he was in the presence of a living saint.

The Superintendent continued. "Everything else is dust. Nothing means anything, but to make it to Heaven. And you're going to make it!"

"But . . . confession. I still want a priest. Please."

"I'll get one. Don't worry. Father Neri won't mind if I wake him up. Then after that . . ." The man faltered, a heavy sigh escaping him. "You can go home. And, to be honest, I'm jealous of you, going home to Our Lord so soon."

Home. The way he said it, a supernatural joy started to burn in Dario's soul, making him suddenly yearn for Heaven. What was it about this man that his words, so simple, could inflame Dario with such peace? Happiness, even? It was like an enormous weight was finally being lifted. And suddenly Dario Tellini felt ready to go to God. Make his confession, then head . . . *home.*

"You'll . . . you'll really wake a priest up for me?"

"Of course I will."

Peace and gratitude flooded Dario's soul. God had sent him a saint to help him in his last hours. How good God was!

Wait. Dario realized something with shock. The Superintendent had called him by his name. More than once. How could he know his name? Dario hadn't told him. Hadn't told Curzio or Bernadino either. No one in this hospital had any way of knowing.

As if reading his mind, the Superintendent said, "You don't recognize me, do you?" His voice, although still strained with pain, held a hint of playful challenge.

Dario studied him in the shadows of the candle and frowned. "No. Should I?"

"I sure hope not. I never again want to be the man you once knew."

With that, the Superintendent of San Giacomo said, "I'll go grab that priest," and rose from his chair.

Up, up, up he went, until he towered above the bed.

The man was a giant.

If you enjoyed this story and would like to revisit the characters, and find out how Camillus went from being a wayward soldier-of-fortune to a holy Soldier of Christ and a canonized saint, you can read the whole story in Susan Peek's novel *A Soldier Surrenders: The Conversion of St. Camillus de Lellis.*

Susan Peek

ABOUT THE AUTHOR

SUSAN PEEK is the author of the young adult series, *God's Forgotten Friends: Lives of Little-known Saints*. All of her novels received the Catholic Writers Guild Seal of Approval and are used in Catholic schools across the English-speaking world. *The King's Prey: Saint Dymphna of Ireland* was voted one of the Top 10 Best Catholic Books of 2017 and *Crusader King* was listed with The 50 Best Catholic Homeschooling Books of 2013. Although Susan's first love is writing for teens, she's also authored several children's books.

Susan is a Third Order Franciscan and mother of eleven children, including two in the Religious life and a son in the U.S. Air Force. She lives in Kansas, where she usually has her nose in a book, finding obscure saints to write about.

You can visit her at www.SusanPeekAuthor.com.

5

SISTER FRANCESCA

by T. M. Gaouette

"My name's Francesca. I'm going to be a nun, so don't fall in love with me." Those were among her first words to me. While most would think them conceited, coming from her lips, they sounded endearing. And as I stood, leaning against the cold brick wall of a dark hall—a hidden hall to the right of the church's sanctuary—the words echoed loud and clear in my thoughts.

I had hidden in the secluded hall to compose myself. But it wasn't working. Memories of her caused my body to heat up and my palms to sweat. I bowed my head, not ready to face the truth. Not ready to see her.

I closed my eyes and remembered the way her face looked the first time we met twelve years ago. She was fourteen years old but mature for her age, and I was a dopey guy of sixteen.

She'd remained kneeling in a pew as my parents and I wedged into the crowd shuffling down the aisle after Mass. As my eyes clung to her, I wondered why I'd never seen her before. Was she new? A white lace mantilla covered her long brown hair, and with bowed head and folded hands, she prayed, oblivious to anyone around her. I held my gaze on her, hating to tear it away. I still had to see her face.

As if she sensed my need, she lifted her chin, and the face of an angel came into view. Then she opened her eyes and looked at me, sending the most amazing zap of electricity through me. It was a life-changing moment for me, but evidently so much less for her, because she closed her eyes again as if she hadn't even seen me.

I felt slighted by this beautiful stranger, but my emotional turmoil was only the beginning.

I noticed her every Sunday following that one, and she was always alone. After Mass, she would walk quickly and silently to her ride—a powder blue seven-speed retro bicycle with a worn flowered basket clasping the front. And then, as I watched with as much discreetness as possible for a boy deeply smitten, she'd tuck her skirt under her, settle on her seat, and peddle away from me for another long, excruciating week.

I finally had the nerve to approach her a few Sundays later while my parents stood outside after Mass talking with Father Brian.

Wandering over to her with extreme caution, I tried to think up a cool and humorous line that would impress. But all my suavity drained from my being, leaving an empty clump of awkwardness, the second she looked up from her bike to watch my approach. My throat tightened.

Before I could back out of my impulsive bravado, I was by her side, asking some ridiculous question about her bike.

"You like my bike?" she responded with the sweetest voice.

"It's very *vintage*," I said, my stare never leaving her green eyes.

"Is that bad?"

"Not at all."

She straightened her leaning bike, and my mind raced to find my next words.

"What's your name? Will you be here next Sunday?" I asked hastily with words drenched in desperation.

And then she spoke the words that would reverberate in my mind forever. "My name's Francesca. I'm going to be a nun, so don't fall in love with me."

I laughed softly at her assurance, continuing to watch as she rode away. Little did I know, she already had me.

She later informed me that she desired to be like Saint Thérèse of Lisieux, because her little ways were so inspiring. And yet this girl had made an impact on me with her own little ways. The way she tucked her hair behind her ear, the way she smiled and her green eyes danced, the way her forehead creased when she couldn't decide whether I was teasing her or being serious. Sometimes, even I didn't know the difference. Oh, and when she said, "Jason," in almost a whisper, I don't think I ever loved my name more.

From that moment on, I called her Sister Francesca but

deeply hoped and even prayed that her devotion, at the very least, was just a façade. Or at the most, could be easily swayed. I'd met many a girl who claimed to follow Christ, but the running joke about Catholic girls—that they didn't act very Catholic, if you know what I mean—was what soured my reputation with many parents in our small New England town. I could get any girl I wanted. The girls knew that. It had something to do with my dark hair, baby browns, and solid physique. Being a quarterback for our high-school team was just an added bonus. I didn't need that, but it sure helped seal the deal.

A fantastic opportunity presented itself one morning after Mass when the gathering clouds unleashed a forceful abundance of raindrops onto our heads. As we all ran to our cars, I turned around and saw Sister Francesca under the sheltered entrance, hugging her arms to her chest and peering up at the darkening sky.

My parents were quick to acquiesce to my request to take Sister Francesca home.

Her face brightened when I rushed through the rain toward her. It was a beautiful sight.

"Can we take you home?" I asked.

She whispered, "Please," and I felt much like a superhero, if truth be told.

So, I wedged her dripping bike into the back of our SUV, and she happily climbed into the backseat next to me.

I had Sister Francesca in the backseat of my parents' car!

While a pitiful start to a relationship—since my parents were sitting in the front—it was a start, regardless.

Sister Francesca wiped her drenched face with her equally drenched hands and squeezed the water from the tips of her hair, all the while smiling and chatting with my folks. She was prettier than ever. It was the best twenty-minute drive I'd ever experienced, out to her country home.

After dropping her off with her bike, my mother was quick to compliment the "pretty girl," from her "sweet face" to her "polite manner."

From then on, my parents were more than happy to take her home whenever she needed it or I found a need. A few times, she even came over for dinner.

She was so amiable and helpful that both my mother and father were smitten with her and the idea that their young Casanova had finally found a sweet, godly girl to hang out with. Although, my mother showed desperate concern that I would "spoil her goodness." Little did she know.

I'd been allowed many times to drive Sister Francesca home after our family dinners, while she raved about how lovely my parents were. But I was constantly distracted by the impending walk to her front door, always hoping, sometimes even praying, that things would be different from the time before.

All my past walks to the door with other willing—and often expectant—girls proved pretty eventful, to say the least, but not with Sister Francesca. With her, my desire exceeded hers to a tremendous degree. In fact, her desire seemed lacking, to my disappointment. She would thank me politely, ask me again to thank my parents, offer me a nod and a smile, and leave me outside her front door, deeply disappointed and desperately wanting.

Sister Francesca, I concluded, would be a hard nut to crack; but in my experience — okay, my *many* experiences — I thought it could be done. I had the eyes, hair, and body, after all. Plus, I had time on my side and girls eager to keep me entertained in the meantime. The problem was that after a few months of getting to know her, my sentiments had done an uncharacteristic and mind-boggling back flip.

Not only was I no longer interested in conquering her, in the crassest of senses, I was no longer interested in conquering any girl. She did that to me. In fact, she had me in a confessional about six months after we met, and I was glad and changed for it. She never insisted I do it, never expected, or even suggested it. She didn't even know about it. Just as she didn't know about the times I'd stop off at the church on my own and kneel before the Lord begging Him to do what He does best. *Make me new again, Lord.*

In knowing her, I was coming to know Him.

She was my motivator, and simply by her presence, she was my strength. Before long, I yearned to be hers, but I had nothing to offer her in return. It was a take, take, take relationship in which I sucked goodness out of her and, oddly enough, I was growing tired of it. What goodness could I inspire in her that she hadn't already perfected in her heart? How could I help someone who already had the Lord as her strength? How could I give back?

It wouldn't be long before my opportunity would reveal itself. It was the day I found out the truth about her father.

While I no longer wanted to conquer her, after less than a year, I did want her to fall desperately in love with me, and time was pressing on. Having failed so far in my efforts to persuade her that she actually loved me, I resolved to invite her on a picnic. It was the last thing I'd have ever suggested in my past life, but in my new one with Sister Francesca, it seemed fitting. She agreed and, to my delight, invited me to her house one Sunday afternoon, even offering to prepare the lunch.

With purple wildflowers in hand and new hope in my heart, I walked up her creaky front porch steps and knocked on the door. She lived in a mustard-yellow farmhouse with a white wraparound porch. As I waited for her to answer the door, the sweet, creamy fragrance of my bouquet flirting with my senses, I gazed at the open field that stretched out in every direction. A moment later, and still no answer, I found myself picking peeling paint from the doorframe.

Finally, the door creaked open and she appeared,

wearing a white short-sleeved cotton dress that fell perfectly below her knees, and making my heart skip a beat. But rather than invite me inside, she glanced back into the dark house and stepped out onto the porch with a picnic basket. Then she closed the door behind her.

My heart sank. "That was sneaky."

"Not really."

"Who do you have hiding in there? A boy?"

"Actually . . . a man."

I stepped back. I was too late.

"Jason, it's my father." Her voice maintained its usual gentle and matter-of-fact tone, but then her soft features creased, and her eyes glistened in the saddest way. "My father's in there all alone in the dark, sitting in a chair, and staring at the wall. Would you like to come in and see?"

I shook my head, lost for words beyond, "I'm sorry." I took the basket from her, and she accepted the bouquet with a sad smile, closing her eyes in the prettiest of ways and inhaling their scent with a soft shaky breath.

Sister Francesca grabbed me by the hand and led me off the porch, around to the back of her house, and into an open meadow of luscious green, sprinkled with vibrant yellows, purples, and orange. She guided me along. I relished the way her small hand wrapped around mine. Finally, she stopped and dropped my hand. Then she turned away and hid her face in her hands. I walked around her until I faced her.

She pressed her fingers against her closed eyes, as if wanting to force the tears to stay in. But they fell anyway.

Her body shook and she grimaced, trying to keep it together.

I'd never witnessed her in a moment of distress, and it cut me all over. Ignoring her rules about touching her, I lowered the basket to the ground and wrapped my arms around her. She sobbed quietly, her body shaking and her soft, rosewater-scented hair pressing against my cheek. I reluctantly pulled away and, with one arm still around her shoulder, picked up the basket and guided her to a giant oak tree a few yards away. I helped her sit down and sat next to her.

"My father's filled with melancholy." She gazed out into the distance, where the colorful meadows kissed the blue sky, and into her own subconscious. "When my mother died three years ago," she said, her voice quivering, "he lost everything." Her pained expression made her seem on the verge of breaking down completely.

"He never lost you." I touched her hair, wanting her so desperately to reach out to me for comfort.

"I lost him." She looked at me, her brow crinkled. "I always hoped that one day I'd come home and he'd be there waiting for me, suddenly back in the world, ready to be my dad again." Her green eyes were flooded again. "Like it used to be." Her bottom lip trembled.

I brushed my thumb on her cheek, catching her tears. "Oh, Sister Francesca, don't cry."

"I can't help it."

We sat there quietly for a long while, gazing out at the landscape. Then she sniffed, let out an unsteady sigh, and began unpacking the picnic basket. I watched her every delicate move. After a whispered blessing, we ate ham and cheese sandwiches and lemon cookies, and drank raspberry iced tea. We hardly spoke, but it was great. I was finally giving. And then later, when the day began to burn out and the sadness about her father had subsided, I looked at her, a hint of selfishness creeping back in.

"You're so pretty. Why would you want to be a nun? You could meet a nice guy, have babies, do something really cool with your life."

"That doesn't sound cool at all." She folded a cloth napkin and packed it into the basket.

"You want to sit in a convent all day and pray? That's it?"

"That's some of it."

"Sounds like a boring life to me."

"Nothing is boring when you're offering it to the Lord."

"But don't you want to fall in love?" This question was specifically for me, but she didn't need to know that.

She smiled, a dreamy look clouding her eyes. "I've already fallen in love."

My heart jumped and a flood of warmth washed over me. I wondered if my cheeks were as flushed as they felt. Then reason took over. What a fool. Of course she'd fallen in love before. Why wouldn't she? How could I have assumed I was the only guy who'd had a deep devotion for her? What a dope.

"Was he in love with you?" I held my breath.

"He is still in love with me."

"I thought you didn't want anyone to fall in love with you?" I couldn't hide the hurt in my voice as I turned away from her.

"That's because my heart is already taken. I'm in love with God, Jason."

I groaned without meaning to before lying back on the cooling grass and peering up through the leafy branches to the late afternoon sky. "Whatever." A short pause followed as my stubborn heart ached.

She said, "Thank you for being such a good friend. Always there for me."

Listening to her words, I turned to her, but all I saw were her glistening green eyes and soft skin. I didn't want to be her friend. I wanted to meet her the rest of the way with a kiss. I lifted myself up on one elbow, coming as close as I could without touching my lips to hers. It wouldn't take much. All I had to do was reach out and bring her an inch closer. Her eyes never left mine. My heart thumped against my ribs, and my body shook.

"Jason, you know if you kiss me, you'll break my heart."

"I've never heard that line before."

She didn't respond. We remained like that for what felt like a whole minute, looking into each other's eyes, frozen in time.

"You really don't want me to kiss you?" I whispered.

"No, I really don't."

"So why don't you move away?"

"Because I'm not the one who needs to."

Another few seconds passed, and I finally released a heavy sigh and lay back down.

She lay down next to me.

If I was to be anything in her life, I'd have to make this about her and not me.

In serving her, I'd be serving Him.

It seemed like we had a lifetime together to talk. We'd found each other. And even though our relationship would never be romantic, we could still be friends. At least, this was what I'd hoped.

But three short months later, I heard the terrible news about her father, although not directly from her. And the next time I saw Sister Francesca, it was at his graveside.

She stood clad in black, her head bowed, and her lips curled down at the corners. Her family, none of whom I recognized, stood around her. When she saw me arrive with my parents, she smiled and her eyes sparkled behind the tears, and again I wished she loved me as much as I loved her.

"I guess people do die of broken hearts," Sister Francesca said.

We stood alone on her porch while the guests mingled inside the house.

"You didn't tell me," I complained.

"I didn't want to burden you with sadness."

Lifting her chin gently with my fingers, I looked into her eyes and whispered, "Burden me."

She looked at me with her sad smile.

I reached for her hand, and she took mine. Then I led her down the steps and to the field. We walked quietly together, both anticipating the question to come. I bit the bullet. I had to know.

"So, what happens now?"

"I leave."

I stopped. I knew it was coming. How could it not? She had no family in the area now, and her only aunt, Aunt Giuseppina, lived in Virginia.

"Jason, our time together is over, and I can't stand that."

I stood facing her, watching her cry for the millionth time that day. She looked her age, so young and vulnerable.

"You know, you could change your mind and marry me." I didn't know where those words came from, but I meant them more than I meant anything I'd ever said to her.

"I'm already married," she said. "Maybe not officially, but I've already given myself to Him." And she smiled. "But I do love you, Jason. You've been such an amazing friend to me. With all my heart, I love you."

"I know you do. And I love you." Oh, how I loved her. I tried to smile through my own tears, but it hurt too much. "I don't suppose you'd let me kiss you, just this one time."

"Oh, Jason," she said, her sob turning into a short laugh. "You *are* persistent, that's for sure." She wiped her tears. "No." She reached out and hugged me. And it was better than any kiss I'd ever had, because I was new again.

In falling in love with her, I'd fallen in love with Him.

Organ music pushed its way through the walls of the church, shunting me eleven years to the present, and waking me from my memories. I tightened my hands into fists and banged my head softly against the brick. If I concentrated, I could smell the sweet scent of rosewater. If I closed my eyes, I could almost hear her voice. If I just left my hiding spot, I could actually see her. I couldn't avoid it any longer anyway, though I wanted to. How desperately I wanted to, because I knew I was about to have my heart broken again.

The church was dimly lit. I was thankful that the organ music drowned the clomping of my footsteps. I looked ahead to the casket, trying not to give away my emotions. Heads turned as I passed. Then, looking down at her, I choked. I felt it in my throat. A giant golf ball-sized lump. My nose stung, my eyes burned. I held onto the side of the casket, my hands gripping onto the cold, hard structure.

Sister Francesca lay inside, looking more beautiful than I'd ever seen her before or could have ever imagined. She still looked like the girl I met years ago, and I suddenly felt like that boy. My chest exploded, beginning from my heart and resonating outward until heat gushed over me and I began to shake. I gripped tighter and held my breath, afraid I'd release a loud aching moan. She seemed to glow, but maybe I just saw her as an angel. She wore a white habit, a veil on her head, and I'd never seen a more beautiful bride. Her hands rested on her chest, a pearl rosary with a gold chain wrapped carefully around her pretty fingers, and she looked as if she were sleeping.

No one knew what Sister Francesca meant to me because I'd never told them. I never really told her. Sure, she thought I had a crush on her, but I don't believe she knew the depth of my devotion. I didn't think it would be fair to share the full truth with her, considering she was giving herself to the Lord with a passion and desire that I had never seen before in a person. She was perfection personified to me, besides Jesus and the Blessed Mother, of course. She was angelic, pure, and no matter how much I had wanted to hold on to her and make her mine, I hadn't wanted to taint who she was. I wanted her to remain that way. I had to let her go then—a higher purpose awaited us both—and I had to let her go again now.

Ironically, Sister Francesca's desire to be like Saint Thérèse of Lisieux had come to pass, and after leaving me broken-hearted, she had moved to Virginia with her aunt and then later had gone on to become a nun at a small, remote convent in the south of France. She lived loving others in her little ways, and then an illness weakened her in her mid-twenties and took her from me. But not before I had a chance to see her this one last time. If only I could have told her what she had done for me. If only I'd had a chance to thank her. I released a shaky sigh and touched her hand.

My sob became a soft laugh as I recalled the many times I'd wished to kiss her but never did because I was afraid she'd hate me for it. She could do nothing now if I leaned in. But I knew she was watching me, the Lord likely by her side, and both shaking their heads at me.

"Sorry," I whispered. "Old habits die hard." Besides, what scandal I would cause among the congregation whose eyes I could feel drilling though my whole being and watching my every move.

"Father?" I felt a gentle tug on my cassock.

The soft whispering voice of an altar boy sounded loud in the now quiet church. I released a steady breath and took another before turning to him.

"We're ready to begin."

I nodded and looked one last time at her.

My name's Francesca. I'm going to be a nun, so don't fall in love with me.

But I had to, Sister Francesca. It was His will. Because in loving you, I was able to find Him. And in finding Him, I just couldn't let Him go.

Bringing characters together from opposite ends of a faith scope often makes for a fun story with surprising twists. This is characteristic of T.M. Gaouette's fiction. For more stories with real characters, exciting twists, draped in God's Mercy, read her *Faith & Kung Fu Series*.

ABOUT THE AUTHOR

T. M. GAOUETTE is the author of the *Faith & Kung Fu* series for young adults, as well as *The Destiny of Sunshine Ranch*. A member of the Catholic Writers Guild, all her novels have received the Catholic Writers Guild Seal of Approval or are in the process. Born in Africa, raised in London, England, Gaouette now lives on a small farm in New England with her husband where she home-schools her four children and raises goats.

A former contributor on Project Inspired, she now writes fiction for teens and young adults. Her desire is to instill the love of God into the hearts of her readers. You can find out more at www.TMGaouette.com.

6

Contemporary

BEHIND THE WHEEL

by Carolyn Astfalk

Sean snatched Dad's car keys from their hook in the mudroom. The clunky *Go Army!* medallion jangled against the keys and then slipped between his sweaty fingers. Thanks to his lightning-fast reflexes, Sean managed to catch the keys with his other hand, only to bobble them twice before they hit the tile floor with a clatter.

Sean froze.

Paul glanced up from where he sat on the living room couch, a slim soft-cover textbook propped against his bent knees. His feet lay on the cherrywood coffee table, dingy socks with worn heels resting on its edge.

Retrieving the keys with one hand, Sean turned to Paul and pressed his index finger to his lips, a signal for his eleven-year-old brother to keep quiet.

Paul's face scrunched in confusion.

A second later, Dad's voice boomed from the front of the house. "I'm going over to Ginny and Joe's now. I'll be back in, uh . . ."

Sean imagined Dad checking his wristwatch,

instantaneously converting *real* time to military time.

The ancient deadbolt on the front door snapped open, and the door whooshed. "By 2200 hours. I want you both in bed. Lights out."

From his spot in the mudroom, Sean peered around the corner and into the living room but only glimpsed Paul bobbing his head.

"Yeah, Dad," Paul mumbled and then dropped his gaze to his book, twisting a lock of his short brown hair around a finger.

Sean stuffed the keys into his front jeans pocket, grabbed his hooded burgundy sweatshirt from a line of hooks inside the door, and tugged it over his head. Glancing at the five-by-seven-inch magnetic mirror affixed to the side of the stackable clothes dryer, he ignored the smudged glass and focused on his reflection.

He ran his fingers through his hair several times until the blond-brown waves fell into place. With the back of his hand, he checked his jawline for signs of stubble, a routine he'd acquired over the last several months.

Still nothing.

He turned his head in either direction, studying his face. Would a little facial hair make a difference? Would Robyn see him as boyfriend material if he had at least the hint of a beard? It seemed she couldn't imagine him as more than a classmate, as if he had the word *sophomore* tattooed across his forehead. His heart thudded in his chest. If he could pull off his plan, she wouldn't write him off as a measly underclassman anymore.

"Where you goin'?" Paul dropped the textbook on the table with a smack.

"Nowhere you need to know about." Sean averted his gaze from the mirror and pulled a pack of breath mints from his hoodie pocket.

Three steps and Paul was in Sean's face. "You're supposed to watch me. Dad said so."

Sean tapped a mint from the case into his palm and held it out to Paul. Could sparkly spearmint in a two-calorie capsule buy his secrecy? Worth a shot. "Want one?"

"No thanks."

With a *suit yourself* shrug, Sean shoved past Paul, ignoring his prior remark, and crossed the room, dodging a haphazard stack of Xbox games and a giant bag of Dad's hiking gear. Body pressed to the cool plaster wall, he pushed aside the living room curtain with a finger. He peered outside and in the direction Dad would've taken walking to Aunt Ginny and Uncle Joe's house three blocks north.

Paul's soft footfalls alerted Sean to his younger brother's approach. "Hey, doofus, Dad didn't give you permission to go anywhere."

Letting the curtain fall, Sean faced Paul, ready to set him straight on how the evening would go down. "I'm taking the truck, and I'm meeting someone."

Paul's expression morphed from startled to confused, his eyes widening. "You don't have a license. Where ya goin'? Who ya meetin'?"

Sean tightened the drawstrings on his sweatshirt, anticipating the bite of a late October evening in northern Maryland. "I'm only going to Rizzo's for a slice. I'll be back in an hour. Way before Dad."

"Are you crazy? You can't drive." Paul raised his hands, palm up, in question. "What if you wreck the truck? And . . . and, you can't just leave me here."

Oh, yes he could. For once, maybe he could go somewhere without Paul tagging along. "What's the matter?" Sean smirked, assessing Paul's still-childlike frame. "You afraid of the bogeyman?"

Hurt flashed in Paul's eyes.

A glimmer of remorse softened Sean's attitude, but he shoved it away. "Listen, it's a piece of pizza, like, ten blocks from here."

"Then why don't you walk?"

Gritting his teeth, Sean strode to the front door. "*Because*, okay? And this is our secret. Ain't nothin' going to happen to Dad's truck. I'll be real careful."

The rumbling bass of a subwoofer rattled the windows as Sean stepped onto the stoop. Clouds obscured the night sky, and a chill dampness signaled rain in the forecast.

Paul followed so closely on his brother's heels that he nearly toppled Sean. "You're only fifteen. Dad'll kill you if he finds out."

With a hand to Paul's chest, Sean pushed him back indoors, into the warm glow of their little red-brick house. The crucifix on the wall above Dad's red leather recliner caught Sean's eye, creating a momentary twinge of guilt that he brushed off with ease. "And that's why you're not gonna tell him."

Sean pulled the door shut, effectively cutting off further conversation. He breathed deeply of the crisp air as he galloped down the steps that led to the driveway.

An image of Robyn as she sat opposite him in the computer lab came to mind. Her shiny golden hair slid over her shoulders as her long, graceful fingers hovered over the keyboard, hunting and pecking. She bit her full pink lips together in concentration, occasionally huffing in frustration.

Neither frustration nor the dim blue glow of the monitor could detract from her beauty. But her looks weren't what drew Sean to her. She saw him. Even what lay deep inside him. He wasn't just a good-looking face to her; he could tell.

Sean had often wise-cracked, "It's tough being as good looking as me," but he winced when the words still slipped from his mouth. He couldn't help that the combination of his cranial features, the set and color of his eyes, and the wave of his hair somehow appealed to girls any more than he could help that a couple of his knuckles double cracked or that his second toe was longer than his big toe. That's the hand he was dealt, like the kids who ended up with raging acne, insane curls, or huge overbites.

He delivered his *good looking* crack in facetious tones because who would ever understand that being attractive could be a burden? It was like complaining you hit the lottery. You shut up and smiled because, by some miracle, you acquired what everyone else wanted. And if there was a downside, you sucked it up and laughed it off.

If it meant a group of girls literally jumped you when you walked onto the playground in fifth grade, so what? When one of said girls pulled your lunch bag out of the trash in seventh grade as a creepy keepsake, you ignored it. And if you had to tolerate a half-dozen girls you barely knew calling your home phone at all hours, getting your dad angry with you, you dealt.

Robyn exhibited no signs of being a body-jumping, trash-picking, phone-calling groupie. She spoke to Sean in the same way she did the other kid she sat opposite in lab—a tall, pale, skinny kid with too-thick glasses and a mystery abscess on his cheek.

If she had a question about their assignment, she asked Sean and actually listened to his answer, challenging him when she disagreed. If he behaved like a jerk, she told him so. And when he did something that impressed her, she told him that, too.

With a glance in either direction to make sure Dad hadn't lingered or turned back, Sean hopped into the pickup truck. He sat low in the seat, stretching his back and neck to peer over the dashboard. The tilt of the mirrors was out of whack, but he didn't dare adjust anything.

He shoved the key into the ignition and turned, his heart pounding as the engine came to life. With a tug, he snapped the seatbelt into place, then laid a hand on the automatic gear shift.

Nervousness swelled in his chest, and he scrunched his

toes and circled his ankle before positioning his right foot over the brake pedal.

You've done this before. No sweat.

He'd driven. Two weeks ago. Dad let him move the truck around in the sprawling driveway at his friend Bob's farmhouse. If he'd spun out of control, skidded, or got the gas pedal stuck, the worst that would've happened was a pancaked chicken.

Stakes were higher tonight.

Wanting to focus all his attention on the road and the two-ton vehicle he now controlled, Sean reached for the volume knob, ready to silence the classic rock blaring from the radio. His hand stilled. What if he forgot to turn it back on later? Dad always played the radio in the car. He'd know.

Glancing in the rearview mirrors and spotting no one, he eased the truck backward. The sun had set, and dusk settled, making it hard to see. He'd have to be extra cautious. He needed the headlights. Now, which knob was it? He braked and searched the dash for a second . . . this one?

He flinched as the windshield wipers moved, stuttering across the dry windshield.

Wrong knob.

There! Off to the side. He flicked the knob, and the headlamps illuminated the garage door.

Breathing a silent prayer, he tapped his foot to the gas pedal.

The truck lurched backward, spitting gravel from

beneath the front tires. Sean slammed on the brakes, jerking to a stop. His heart settled several seconds after the vehicle.

Motion in the living room window caught his attention. Paul, a stupid grin on his face, pointed. Then, as if anticipating Sean's irritation, let the curtain fall.

Sean exhaled and returned his foot to the gas pedal, pressing more gently this time.

With little effort, he backed the truck into the street, narrowly avoiding Mrs. Booth's trash can. A sporty little black car zipped up behind him, its lights shining brightly in Sean's mirrors. Fumbling with the gear shift, Sean waved the car around. Last thing he wanted was to rush and make a stupid mistake.

The most direct route to Rizzo's would take him past Aunt Ginny and Uncle Joe's, so he devised an alternate route. Though he was grateful for Dad's absence tonight, the seemingly urgent family meeting left Sean puzzled.

Dad had been tense lately, quieter and more withdrawn. He wasn't what you'd call a talkative guy to begin with, but for the past couple of weeks, Sean and Paul had gotten no more than cursory words from him. "Good morning." "How was school?" "What time should I pick you up?" "Is your homework done?"

Dad had been at the computer more, too, looking stuff up. Typically he complained about technology, urging Sean and Paul to get away from the screen. But lately he'd been hogging all the time at the keyboard.

Yeah, something was up with Dad. Something he

wasn't willing to share with Sean and Paul. But maybe with Aunty Ginny and Uncle Joe? They'd been the ones to hold the family together when Mom had died years ago.

As Sean rolled down the street, his mind ticked through the possible reasons for Dad's reticence.

A silver minivan pulled out from a side street right in front of him.

Sean's thoughts scattered. He gripped the wheel and slammed on the brakes. Something in the bed of the truck thudded and rolled; he had no idea what.

The minivan sped on its way. Sean sucked in a breath, praying he'd make it to the pizza shop with the truck unscathed. Maybe this hadn't been such a great idea.

Ten minutes later, turn signal clicking over the sounds of the Steve Miller Band, Sean turned the truck smoothly into the parking lot in front of a small strip mall. Rizzo's occupied the end property, its red lettering and neon pizza slice advertising its presence.

Scoping out the lot, Sean spied a patch of empty spaces at the far side where other businesses had closed for the day. Sweat gathered under his arms and behind his neck. Now would be a good time for his video game skills, well-honed behind a virtual steering wheel, to kick in. He pulled in, backing up twice and pulling forward to re-center the vehicle between the white lines.

He shoved the gear shift into park, and a huge weight lifted from his shoulders. He'd arrived. Tapping his fingers on the wheel, he honed in on the singer's voice. Was he singing about smoking pot? What the heck did Dad listen to anyway?

Once Sean had turned off the engine and applied the emergency brake—the lot was level, but just in case—he peered over his shoulder. Inside the front window of Rizzo's, in an orange booth beneath a cheap Tiffany-style lamp, sat Robyn.

A clip of some kind held her long, blonde hair in place at the back of her head, and she sipped from a straw. A book lay open in front of her.

He smiled, biting his bottom lip as a wave of nerves hit him. Right where she said she'd be.

Not that she'd be expecting him.

She'd told Abscess Cheek she hung out at Rizzo's on Thursday nights from seven o'clock to eight-thirty while her younger sister was in ballet class at the studio across the street. Her mom worked that night, and her dad had to get her little brothers into bed, leaving her to chauffeur duty.

Sean exited the truck and crossed the parking lot, a skip in his step as he mounted the sidewalk. Excitement and nervousness pulsed through his veins. Once Robyn saw him outside of school, on his own, having driven here himself, she wouldn't care that he—

The front of his tennis shoe caught on a rise in the pavement, and he stumbled forward. His feet pedaled ahead two paces before his palms landed flat against the window pane, one on either side of Robyn's seat.

She jerked back, bumping her drink, which toppled and spilled across the tabletop and onto her book. Brown liquid, probably a Coke, puddled around the condiment tray as she slid her paperback out, shaking it gently.

Sean visualized the SAT vocabulary words on the left hand side of the white board in his American Lit class. He ticked through them mentally until he landed on the most apropos one, which then flashed before him.

M-O-R-T-I-F-I-E-D

"In a sentence please, Mr. Porter."

"Mortified. I was mortified when I stumbled and flattened myself onto a pane of glass in front of the only girl I ever cared to impress. Mortified."

Swallowing the lump of humiliation clogging his throat, Sean straightened and reached for the door handle. Bells jingled overhead as he rounded the table and darted for Robyn. On his way, he yanked a fistful of napkins from the metal dispenser and blotted what he could of the sticky, liquid mess on the table.

"Hey, Robyn. I, uh—"

"Did you have a nice trip?" Mischievous amber eyes peeked from beneath long brown lashes lightly coated in mascara. A smile inched wider, dimpling her cheeks despite her having to sop up a pile of shaved ice that melted and dripped onto the booth seat beside her. Her suppressed laughter erupted in a snort, dissolving the knot that had built in his chest.

"Yeah, it was a doozy. Enjoying your beverage?"

She snorted a second time, an endearing, feminine noise despite its similarity to a swine's signature sound.

He pushed their combined pile of sopping napkins to

the center of the table. "Mind if I sit down?"

"Nope. As long as you promise not to make me topple any more drinks." She dried her hand on a clean napkin and examined her book, which, surprisingly, looked no worse for wear.

"Sorry about that." Disaster averted, or at least contained, a chasm of silence opened between them filled only by Nickelback's "Rockstar" coming from the speaker overhead.

"I hate this song." Robyn folded her hands atop her book, waiting, it seemed, for Sean to steer the conversation.

"Yeah, me too. So, uh, you like this place?" He jerked a thumb toward the counter where a portly middle-aged man in a white tee shirt slid a paper plate of greasy deep dish toward a customer. With it came a fresh wave of the aroma of tomato sauce and oregano.

She shrugged, then tapped a fingernail against the window, pointing at the single-story building across the street. "My little sister is at Dancing Queens. I'd rather sit here than in the waiting room over there. Stinks like sweaty girls and cherry lip gloss." She wrinkled her nose.

Sean laughed. "Gotcha."

Fifty minutes later, his cheeks aching from smiling so hard, Sean stood as Robyn slid out of her side of the booth. A steady stream of little girls in pink tutus poured out of the studio across the street, dragging their pink satin ballet bags behind them.

"You're good company, Sean Porter." She slid a phone

from her tiny purse. "Text me your number?" She glanced down, her cheeks growing pink.

Elation, chased by humiliation, had Sean scrambling for a response. He had to be the only teen in a thirty-mile radius without a phone. As per Dad's rules. He'd promised Sean a flip phone, once he got his driver's license.

"Uh, sorry." He jammed his hands into his pockets, unsure what to say or do next. "No phone."

"Oh." In a half second, she recovered from her surprise and grabbed the last clean napkin from the center of the table. Pulling a purple gel pen from her purse, she scribbled on the napkin, folded it in half, and handed it to him. "There."

He accepted the napkin, his fingers brushing hers. Sean pressed it carefully into his back pocket, resisting the desire to immediately read what she'd written. "I'll walk you out."

Outside the door, breaks in the traffic revealed the sound of crickets chirping. Moths swirled overhead, bumping into the lights.

At Robyn's car, Sean said, "Well, see ya at school tomorrow."

Robyn fiddled with her car keys, smiling. "See ya."

Sean nearly floated to the truck.

With the door firmly shut and seatbelt in place, he let loose possibly the biggest smile ever. A fresh boost of confidence kept worries of the drive home at bay. He glanced at the dashboard clock. Plenty of time to get back before Dad.

Outside his window, cars continued to file out of the dance studio lot. Sean backed the truck up, grateful he'd parked on the empty side of the lot, and eased to the exit.

He smothered his smile—he'd think about Robyn later, probably all night. For now, he needed to block out the ZZ Top track on the radio and concentrate on the road. Using the turn signal, he turned left. He immediately slowed in front of the dance studio as a family stepped onto the crosswalk.

A girl of about seven or eight in the requisite pink tutu ran ahead while a mother with a toddler clinging to each hand followed. They'd stepped onto the curb in front of Rizzo's, when another kid, a boy who looked to be Paul's age, sprinted across behind them.

Headlights flashed, temporarily blinding Sean, as a small black SUV barreled toward him in the opposite lane. With horror, Sean anticipated what was about to happen.

A collision was imminent.

Pressing frantically on the center of the steering wheel, he tried to activate the horn. He glanced down, finally discovering the little horn image, and laid on it. Too late.

Brakes squealed, but the SUV clipped the kid's heel, knocking him forward.

Eyes wide with shock, Sean sat transfixed. A moment later, he blinked out of his stupor and took in the scene.

The mother had left the toddlers in the hands of the tutu girl as she dropped to the pavement in front of the motionless boy.

The SUV remained still, the driver making no attempt to exit the car. In the dark, Sean couldn't even make out whether it was a guy or a woman. The passenger's side of the front bumper didn't appear dented, but the decorative plate in the center depicting palm trees silhouetted in front of a golden sunset and the name *Stewarts* hung askew.

Suddenly, the vehicle jerked backward, then raced forward and down the street.

The white tee guy from Rizzo's and several patrons rushed out to help the injured boy and the woman leaning over him.

Sean gulped, his stomach twisting. He'd driven slowly and carefully, obeying all the rules of the road—aside from the one about possessing a license. And yet, he'd been witness to an accident not of his doing.

The perpetrator had sped off. Maybe he should too. He wasn't at fault.

But he'd been a witness.

With his hands settled on the steering wheel, knuckles white, he eyed the empty road ahead. Nothing to stop him from proceeding home, same as he'd come. It'd been a good night. Robyn liked him, despite the fact he was an underclassman and not because of how he looked. They'd enjoyed being together.

In a few minutes, he could be home. There'd even be time for him and Paul to go over homework or watch something before bed.

He pressed his fingers against his eyes and then massaged his forehead, knowing the right thing to do.

Sirens wailed in the distance as Sean backed up—flashers on, slowly and carefully—into what was probably the worst parallel park job known to man. A minute later, when the flashing lights of a police car reflected in his rearview mirror, he steeled his courage and begged God not only for the health of the injured kid but to get him through this mess. Preferably without Dad knowing.

After more police officers and EMTs arrived, taking stock of the victim and the traffic situation, Sean exited the truck, patting the rear pocket where he carried his student ID and Robyn's napkin.

Swallowing hard and mustering his courage, he approached a stocky young police officer standing alongside his vehicle at the edge of the scene. "Excuse me, officer. I witnessed the accident." The wind kicked up, scattering dry leaves that had gathered along the berm. "I can give you a description of the vehicle that hit the kid."

Forty minutes later, that same police officer pulled his cruiser in front of the Porter home. From behind the curtain, warm light shone through the living room window. Sean glanced at the dashboard clock. A good twenty minutes shy of 2200 hours, so Dad wouldn't—

The front door swung open, and Dad stepped onto the porch, hands on his hips, a scowl on his face.

Sean's stomach flipped.

Appropriately chastened, he thanked the officer for driving him home and exited the vehicle, a copy of the fine he'd been issued firm in his hand.

The police cruiser pulled away before either he or his father had taken a step. Time to man up, face the music, put on his big boy pants, pay the piper, or whatever other cliché fit plunging headlong toward imminent doom. At this rate, he wouldn't get his driver's license until he was eighteen. Let alone a cell phone.

Sean climbed the steps as if someone had attached leaden weights to his tennis shoes. At the first landing, he stopped and chanced a look at Dad. He'd never felt smaller or weaker in his life.

Dad's gaze roamed Sean's body from head to foot. Seemingly satisfied that he hadn't been hurt, Dad's gaze hardened to a glare. "Care to explain where you've been and where my truck is?"

In this case, Sean knew the honest answer, "No thanks, I'm headin' to bed," wouldn't mollify his father, although the retort tempted him. "Sure, Dad," came out of his mouth instead as he crossed in front of his father, a hard stare warming Sean's ears and tightening his gut.

Inside the house, Paul backed away from the window where he'd apparently been lurking and skittered to the farthest seat on the couch.

"Snitch," Sean mouthed, regretting it immediately. Paul was just a kid. It hadn't been fair to ask him to keep his secret. What if Sean'd been the one lifted into an ambulance outside of Rizzo's? His little brother shouldn't have that on his conscience.

The door slammed and the dead bolt snapped shut.

"Sit," Dad barked in his formidable Army voice that never failed to garner the Porter boys' full and undivided attention.

Sean obeyed for the first time that night, and sat, letting his head droop. Finally, uncomfortable silence forced his gaze up.

"I got the gist of what you planned from Paul." Dad glanced at Paul, whose sagging expression said he was ashamed of his complicity. "He called me when you were gone later than you said you'd be. Let's hear the rest."

Sean released the fine he'd crumpled in his sweaty palm and flattened it on the table. Then he explained his trip to Rizzo's and the hit-and-run he'd witnessed while leaving.

Dad sucked in a deep breath and exhaled, looking as if he'd aged a decade over the course of the evening. How long had he had those creases in his forehead and that sprinkling of gray in his hair? He fiddled with his bare ring finger, his trademark tell for when he especially missed Mom.

Despite looking angrier than Sean had ever seen him, Dad pretty much kept his cool as he spent the next who-knew-how-many minutes rehashing what Sean had done wrong: disobeying the law and Dad, endangering himself and others, shirking his responsibility to Paul and expecting him to cover for him. All of which Sean knew — and had known, intellectually — before he'd ever pocketed the keys. At the time, it'd all seemed inconsequential, a distant second to earning the attention and affection of a junior girl with amber eyes who seemed to understand there might be more to Sean than even he had recognized.

Eventually, Dad's lecture wound to a close, leaving Sean doleful and disappointed in himself.

Apparently, Paul lacked both the patience and the sense to wait more than two silent beats before chiming in. "Can someone go over this religion stuff with me? I've got a test tomorrow."

Dad tilted his head from side to side, as if working out the kinks, then massaged the back of his own neck. "This is *not* how I expected this evening to go." He extended a hand toward Paul, palm up. "Let's have a look."

Paul handed him the open book and poked a finger at the page. "This stuff, here."

Dad's gaze roamed over the page for several seconds. "Gifts of the Holy Spirit. Go."

Sean stood, eager to escape to the shower, where he could decompress. Taking the truck, meeting Robyn, the accident, Dad finding out—he needed time to process it all. The police officer had assured him the kid hit by the SUV sustained only minor injuries, but it still had him shaken. He made it only two strides toward the hall and the bathroom.

"Take a seat," Dad bellowed from where he stood opposite the couch. With his free hand, he swiped the crumpled fine from the table and let it flutter back down. "We're not done. There's still your punishment to discuss."

Sean sighed, careful not to let his exasperation show,

and slumped back to the couch.

Attention shifted to Paul again, Dad waiting for his recitation.

Eyes squeezed shut, Paul began. "Wisdom, knowledge, counsel . . ." He tapped a fist against his palm. "Uh, piety. Fortitude."

"Stop." Dad's gaze wandered the page again. "Define fortitude."

"Uh, courage," Paul said with a note of uncertainty.

Dad nodded then read from the page margin: "Virtue that ensures firmness in difficulties. Strengthens the resolve to resist temptations, overcome obstacles. Enables one to conquer fears, face trials and persecution." The book smacked shut, and Dad placed it on the table.

"Despite what happened," he leveled a pointed look at Sean, "I've seen evidence of fortitude in both of you tonight. Paul, you called me when you knew you'd be in trouble with both me and Sean. Because it was the right thing to do."

Paul swallowed and gave the slightest nod.

"And Sean," he said, shaking his head, "Well, you did the right thing too, sticking around and going to the police when you knew it would get you in trouble with them and with me."

Sean sat straighter in his seat, eager for the smallest scrap of respect Dad proffered.

"So . . ." Dad moved the coffee table away from the couch and sat on it. He leaned forward, resting his elbows on his knees. "I need to show some fortitude too. We're all gonna need a hefty dose of it, so we better start praying to the Holy Spirit."

Sean's brow wrinkled. What did he mean? Why did they need fortitude? What about understanding? Sean liked that gift. Didn't seem to require much on his part.

Dad bit his lips together and dropped his gaze to his hands. "I'm being deployed." Dad made eye contact first with Paul, then Sean, his firm gaze communicating the seriousness of his words. "I leave in five weeks for Afghanistan. You'll be staying with Aunt Ginny and Uncle Joe while I'm gone."

Sean's breathing stalled. "How long—?"

Dad held up a hand, silencing Sean. "I know you've got a lot of questions. I wish I had answers, but I don't. Very few."

Paul launched himself from the couch into Dad's arms, his cheeks already wet with tears.

Dad squeezed him, reassuring him that everything would be okay. Once Paul settled, Dad dismissed him to get ready for bed.

With a grim smile, Dad motioned for Sean to come closer until he sat opposite him. "No Xbox until further notice."

"Okay." Was that it? Sean expected worse. Cleaning out the garage. Chopping off a limb. Something.

"Are we good?"

Sean nodded. Despite wanting to keep his cool, tears built behind his eyes, closing his throat. He glanced down the hall, hoping Paul would hurry it up so he could take refuge in the shower. Tonight had been enough; he couldn't even think about his dad going to war. Wouldn't think about it. Not yet.

Dad's chin dipped. "You sure?"

"Yeah," Sean croaked. "Can I go to my room now?"

Dad didn't answer right away, his gaze boring into Sean. "Go ahead."

Relieved, Sean swallowed his emotion and strode to the hall.

"Sean," Dad called.

He stopped, but didn't turn, hoping whatever Dad had to say wouldn't take long.

"I love you."

Sean's breath hitched. "You too, Dad."

Flopping belly first on the bed, Sean finally relaxed. A few tears fell, but not the torrent he expected. He wiped his eyes on the back of his arm and let his thoughts drift, listening for the shower to stop, signaling his turn in the bathroom.

An image of Robyn sopping up her spilled Coke popped into his mind, and he managed a smile. Oh—the napkin she'd given him! He still hadn't looked at it.

He slid the napkin from his rear pocket and unfolded it. Once. Twice.

In purple gel ink, she'd scratched a couple of lines. She hadn't bothered with the phone number, he guessed since he didn't have a phone of his own. Wasn't like he couldn't use the home phone, though.

Diagonally across the napkin, she'd written: "I like a

guy with guts, even if he's a klutz." At the end of the sentence, she drew a smiley face.

Sean grinned. Guts, huh? *Fortitude*. He'd take it.

Follow "Behind the Wheel" characters Sean and Paul Porter in the coming-of-age story for older teens and adults, *Rightfully Ours*, when their dad's second deployment uproots their lives, taking them far from home.

Carolyn Astfalk

ABOUT THE AUTHOR

CAROLYN ASTFALK writes from The Sweetest Place on Earth, Hershey, Pennsylvania, where she lives with her husband and four children. In addition to her contemporary Catholic romances (sometimes referred to as Theology of the Body fiction), including the young adult coming-of-age story *Rightfully Ours*, she writes for CatholicMom.com and *Today's Catholic Teacher*. When she's not washing dishes, doing laundry, or reading, you can find her blogging about books, family life, and faith at www.CarolynAstfalk.com.

7

MORE PRECIOUS THAN GOLD

by Leslea Wahl

MONDAY

The clock is ticking. We don't have much time. My heartbeat hammers frantically from the stress. I'm searching everywhere but can't find the key. It's got to be here. I yank open the drawers again; maybe I missed something. No. It can't end like this—we're too close. But as the moments tick by, I'm afraid we're doomed.

"Ryan! Hurry!" My hands shake as panic surges through me.

He's fiddling with a combination lock, trying a series of numbers, desperate to unlock the safe.

"Hurry, they'll be here any second!" I hear footsteps in the hallway.

With one last spin of the dial, the metal door swings open. There it is, sitting on a stack of yellowing papers. The key to our freedom. I snatch it and race to the far door.

With my hand trembling, I can't quite insert the key.

"Josie, let me help."

Ryan comes up behind me, his steady hand guiding the key into the lock. Together we turn the key. An audible click. The door opens.

"We did it! We escaped!" Relief pours through me.

From around the corner, a big burly man emerges. His eyes bore into us. We watch him carefully, unsure of our next move.

"Congratulations. You escaped." He displays about as much enthusiasm as a cat sunning itself. "You can pick up your certificate in the office."

"We did it!" I wrap my arms around Ryan.

Ryan grins at the guy, whose eyebrows are raised, quite literally looking at me like I'm insane. "She's always wanted to try one of these escape rooms."

I nod. "We don't have any cool escape rooms in our town so, since we were coming up to Minneapolis to pick up relatives at the airport, we thought we'd try one."

The answering yawn makes me suspect he doesn't really care.

"You're the first ones to come in costume." He scans our 1920s attire.

"Really? That's part of the fun." I do a few quick twists, the fringe of my flapper dress swaying with the movement.

The guy glances back at Ryan. "You've got a unique girl there."

"Don't I know it." Ryan pulls me close, kissing my

cheek. I can't get over how cute he looks in his fedora. A themed escape room is, of course, a perfectly appropriate place to wear a fedora.

"Well. Good job." He gives us a half-hearted thumbs-up, then wanders back down the hall.

"Now you can cross that off your bucket list." Ryan glances at his watch. "Okay, we better change. We need to get to the airport."

"So, tell me about your cousin." Fearing I'll be swept away by the wave of newly arrived passengers, I cling to Ryan's hand.

We're about to spend a week of the summer before our senior year helping at a summer camp for disadvantaged kids. Ryan has been a counselor there before, but this will be my first time, and I have a major case of stage fright. Not only will we be working with these kids, who I'm not sure I'll connect with, but Ryan's cousin and her boyfriend are flying in from Colorado to volunteer as well. I've heard a lot about this favorite cousin of his and really want to make a good impression.

"Sophie's cool, we've always had fun together."

"What's her boyfriend's name again?"

"Jake."

When his face brightens with a smile, I turn to see a girl our age with wavy brown hair hurry towards him. A gorgeous dark-haired guy follows her. We're talking drop-dead gorgeous.

"Ryan!" Her arms wrap around him.

"Hey, Soph. This is my girlfriend, Josie."

I glance at her but turn my attention back to the guy next to her. I don't mean to stare but can't help it. His movie star looks are like a magnet for the eyes.

"Ryan, Josie, this is my boyfriend, Jake."

Jake flashes a high-wattage smile my way. When recognition hits, the blood seems to drain from my body. *Do not faint.* I turn towards Ryan and punch his arm.

"Seriously, Ryan? You never thought to tell me that your cousin is dating Jake Taylor. *The* Jake Taylor?"

He shrugs with one of his signature grins. "Guess it slipped my mind."

"It slipped your mind that she's dating a famous, silver-medal winning snowboarder?"

When people around us turn to stare, I realize I may have screeched that information a little too loudly. People begin pointing and pulling out their phones. One young boy asks for an autograph. I notice a slight twitch of Jake's jaw before he graciously agrees. Soon a line of fans forms.

Oops. I hadn't meant to make a scene thirty seconds after we met.

I turn to Ryan. "This is your fault. Why didn't you warn me?"

His grin deepens. "I thought the element of surprise might be more fun."

Sophie rolls her eyes at him, then we both punch his arms.

After finally pulling Jake away from the madness, we

load Ryan's SUV and hit the road.

The seatbelt strains against me as I turn in my seat to chat with Jake and Sophie. "Again, sorry I directed so much attention at you."

"Josie's specialty is creating interesting situations." Ryan shoots me a wink.

Sophie smiles. "And here I thought musical theater was your specialty."

Does she think that's a bad thing? Her tone reveals nothing. "They tend to go hand in hand. My theatrical side sometimes makes life interesting. But really, I'll try to keep my fangirl excitement suppressed."

Jake shrugs. "No worries. Being recognized is an occupational hazard."

"I can't wait to tell my friend Liz that I met you. She's quite obsessed, even has one of your calendars hanging on her bedroom wall." I force my eyes off his face. Ogling the guy is probably not the way to make a good impression.

"A lot of people like his calendar," Sophie states, a slight edge to her voice.

"But not everyone." Jake nudges his girlfriend.

"You didn't like it?" Hard to believe.

She glances out the window then back at me. "Sure, it was great, but the thought of pictures of your boyfriend hanging on bedroom walls across America is a little disconcerting."

Ryan laughs and shoots Sophie a look through the rearview mirror. She playfully scowls. Their interaction makes me pretty sure I'm missing some kind of inside joke.

"Changing the subject here." She flicks his head with her finger. "How'd the baseball season go, Ryan?"

"Good."

I roll my eyes at him. "Don't let him fool you. It was amazing. He was named one of Minnesota Youth Athletes to Watch."

"Wow, that's awesome, man." Jake pats Ryan's shoulder. "It's nice to finally meet you. Sophie talks about you a lot."

As he switches lanes, Ryan looks over his shoulder. "I bet she made me out to be the cousin that always pulled pranks on her."

"Yeah, something like that."

"Well, watch your back, man. She may look sweet and innocent, but she has a devious side. Did she ever tell you about the time our families went to Mackinaw Island and she buried me in the sand, leaving only my head exposed, then disappeared, leaving me trapped?"

Yeesh! Not sure about their idea of fun.

Sophie laughs. "Oh, poor Ryan. That was just retaliation for him convincing me the weird seaweed on the beach was good for my hair. He watched me braid the slimy strings into my hair and everything. Then it dried. Ugh." Her face crinkles like she can still smell it. "Took days to wash the stench out."

Should be an interesting week with these two.

The car slows, jarring me awake. We turn onto a road

lined by thick, towering trees. Eventually the dense forest opens up, revealing the camp. Log cabins and a dirt ball field are nestled beside a shimmering lake. Rocks and pines surround the picturesque setting.

The camp director, Paul, scurries out of the main lodge to greet us. "Welcome!"

After a quick tour around the camp, we turn back toward the main lodge, which looks like one of my brother's Lincoln Log creations.

"I'm glad you all could join us. The mission of this camp is to provide an opportunity for disadvantaged kids to experience nature in a Christian environment. We try not only to instill in them the love of God, but also help them see they all have amazing gifts and talents they can use to improve their lives. Growing up in desperate situations can lead kids to all kinds of problems like joining gangs, dropping out of school, and drug use. The kids at this camp are only in fifth and sixth grades, but some are tough nuts to crack." He runs his hand through his hair. "As you know, the kids have been here a few days already. There's one boy in particular, Jet, I'm worried about. He could really use some positive role models. His older brother, who was actually trying to make a better life for himself, was killed recently in gang violence. We've been trying hard to reach him."

"How horrible." I glance at Ryan. Is it too late to back out? I'm not sure I'm cut out for this.

We follow Paul inside the lodge. "I've assigned some tasks that I hope will be fun and can utilize your own gifts.

Sophie, your writing and photography skills are impressive. Would you mind taking photos this week? I'm hoping to update our brochures and website this fall."

She smiles. "That sounds fantastic."

"Josie, I hear you're an actress. Would you coordinate the talent show for Friday evening?" He nods towards a small stage at the far end of the room.

"Absolutely!" Thank goodness. I was afraid I'd have to do something out of my comfort zone this week, like rock climbing or knot tying. Talent show? Piece of cake.

As Paul tells the guys their jobs for the week, the lure of the stage draws me closer.

Ideas for an opening production number flit through my mind when I notice a boy slumped against the side of the stage, next to the piano. His matted hair shoots from his head in a million directions, resembling a dirty mop. His serious, big brown eyes watch me from his grimy face.

"Hi. I'm Josie."

When he doesn't answer, I decide a prompt might be necessary.

"This is the point in the conversation where you're supposed to tell me your name."

"Why?"

"Because." Little does he know, I have a younger brother. There is no way this little twerp is getting the best of me.

After a short stare down, where he must realize I'm not budging, he sighs. "It's Jet."

Oh, so this is the boy Paul mentioned.

"Cool name. It reminds me of *West Side Story*. The Jets and the Sharks were rival gangs."

His expression hardens even more. "What do you know about gangs?"

Shoot. I spoke before thinking *again*. Paul just told us his brother had been killed by gang violence. Off to a stellar start. I close my eyes. *Hey God, I could use a little help here.*

"You're right. I don't know much about gangs, but it's still a good musical."

He rolls his eyes. "A musical about gangs? That's dumb."

"Hey mister," I teasingly scold. "No dissing Broadway musicals unless you've seen them."

The corner of his mouth twitches. Did he almost smile?

"Let me guess, you're here to try and save kids like me." He rubs his chin, smearing dirt along his jawline.

"Nope, just here to produce the most amazing summer camp talent show west of the Mississippi. I don't suppose you'd like to help me?"

"Why would I want to do that?"

I cross my arms. "I don't know. Because it might be more fun than staring into space. But, hey, your loss if you don't want to participate."

With a shrug I walk towards an old stereo along the adjacent wall, but from the corner of my eye I see him watching me.

TUESDAY

After spending all morning with the rambunctious campers, the four of us find ourselves with a little free time. It couldn't have come at a better time. There is not enough caffeine in all of northern Minnesota to help me match the energy level these kids possess.

Ryan's thrilled to lead us on a hike to show us his favorite spots. This whole outdoorsy thing is not really in my repertoire, so I couldn't care less about this hike, but I am excited for the chance to get to know Jake and Sophie better. Ever since I knew we would all be working here, I had envisioned Sophie and myself sprawled out on our bunk beds, sharing secrets, and chatting late into the night. But, in reality, we were both exhausted last night and fell right to sleep. Today, we might finally have a chance to bond.

"This camp is great, Ryan." Sophie pulls out her ever-present camera to capture a view of the valley, peeking from between the trees. She adjusts the lens. "Did you happen to notice the sign at the bottom of that hill? 'Isabelle's Peak.' I've noticed a lot of unusually-named locations around here. Do you know the story behind them?"

"Sorry, never noticed." Ryan grips my arm to steady me when I trip on a root invading my path.

"How could you not wonder about places named Lovers Leap, Heartbreak Hollow, and Fugitive Forest?" Her voice rises.

"Um, because they're just names?"

Sophie stops walking and looks at him like he just said the most ridiculous thing. "Even this camp's name—Camp Mercy—is intriguing. Don't you know there are stories behind the names?"

His hands shoot up in surrender. "Honestly, never thought about it."

"Don't worry, pal." Jake gives him a sympathetic look. "I never knew that either, but your lovely cousin has a knack for uncovering these kinds of things."

"Learn something new every day. There's a little library in town, maybe they can fill you in."

As we continue, Ryan and Jake lag behind, deep in a conversation about rock climbing. Does anyone besides them care about bouldering and belaying? I think not. Sophie is distracted by all the flowers along the path and keeps snapping photos of them. Which puts me in the lead. I harness my inner Maria from *Sound of Music*, ready to climb every mountain. But somehow I must've made a wrong turn. Two giant stones tower over us, blocking the path.

Ryan nudges me with his shoulder. "Think we hit a dead end."

"So much for my mountaineering skills."

Sophie wanders closer to the formation. A narrow passage between the stones makes it look like they were once one massive rock that split in two. "This is fantastic. I wonder if these rocks are named?"

A quick scan reveals nothing. "I don't see a sign. Maybe

you can name it yourself."

"How about Two Giant Rocks?" Ryan not-so-helpfully suggests.

The look Sophie shoots him reveals just how unamused she is. "You don't get this naming thing, do you? The name has to have meaning, a story behind it."

"Okay, how about the Josie Got Us Lost Rock. Is that descriptive enough?"

My turn to shoot him a dirty look. So hilarious.

"How about Minnesota Stonehenge?" Jake grins.

"No, wait!" I add, inspiration hitting. "Sophie's Stonehenge."

She rolls her eyes. "I think you guys are possibly the worst site-naming team in history."

"Hate to cut our excursion short." Ryan glances at his watch. "We've got to head back. Jake and I are the captains of the teams for this afternoon's kickball game. You girls want to cheer us on?"

"Sure!" I jump on his back for a piggy-back ride. He can lead the way this time.

Sophie's gaze lingers on the rock. "I'm sure you'll have enough fans there without me. I'm going into town to find out more about the names of all these sites."

Jake tugs a strand of her hair. "Our intrepid investigative reporter has a new story to chase."

"I'll go with you." I blurt out. "A girls' day out will be fun."

An unsure look passes over Sophie's face, which makes my insides drop, but she answers graciously. "Sure, the company would be great. We'll meet you guys back at the lodge for dinner."

Finally, the perfect opportunity to get to know her better.

As we exit the hiking path on our way to camp we come across a lone boy sitting in the dirt, staring towards the ball field. Jet. The guys approach him. Hopefully they'll have more luck than I did.

Ryan squats down next to him. "Hey, Jet."

Jet's intense stare settles on Ryan's face, but he doesn't respond.

"Want to join us? I could use a strong kid on my team." Jake kneels as well.

The boy scoops up dirt in his hands then watches it filter through his fingers. "No."

"That's because he wants to join me on the winning team," Ryan jokes.

The cold annoyance turns to a fiery scowl, his wrath aimed at Jake. "Why are you even here? You're rich and famous. Why would you waste your summer with a bunch of loser kids? Does it make you feel better about yourself?"

Yikes.

Jake closes his eyes for a moment then turns to Jet. "You're right, I have been pretty lucky in my life. You know what my favorite part of fame is? It's the chance to share my belief that God gave us all amazing gifts and talents. I'm sure you have some pretty cool interests or skills. The key is finding a way to use those interests to help others."

A shadow passing over his face, Jet clenches his grimy fist. "My brother thought that too. Lot of good that did him. It's better to play the cards you're dealt and forget your dreams, or you'll end up dead."

I wince. If the guys can't reach him, who can? We may need some divine intervention.

Ryan runs his hand through his hair. "You know, I can't really relate to what you've been through. Horrible things happen, and I'm so sorry you lost your brother, but maybe you have a chance to fulfill his dreams now."

"Whatever. Just leave me alone." Jet glares off in the distance, shutting everyone out.

Jake stands. "Hey, man, if you ever want to talk, you know where you can find us."

With that, the guys head towards the ball field. As Sophie and I make our way to the parking lot, I pray that someone this summer will be able to reach that kid.

When the boys come into the dining hall to join us for dinner, I can hardly keep my excitement in check. "Wait till you hear! It's so exciting! This camp has a secret."

Ryan lifts his eyebrows at my exuberance.

"Wait," Sophie says. "What happened?"

My enthusiasm caused me to miss the obvious. They're both limping and covered in dirt. Dried blood is smeared across Ryan's arm.

Jake slumps onto the bench next to Sophie. "The kickball game was a little intense."

I search Ryan's face, exhaustion making his features droop. "Playing kickball with a bunch of kids was that grueling?"

An indiscernible look passes between the guys.

Sophie's eyes narrow. "You guys are athletes; a friendly ball game shouldn't have been that difficult."

"Tell your cousin that." Jake rests his head on his hand.

A slight grin forms on Ryan's tired face. "It kinda turned into a battle. Neither of us wanted to lose, so we played a little rougher than necessary. When the kids noticed, they joined in the intense matchup. At one point, I beamed the ball at Jake as he tried to steal second."

Jake grimaces. "Yeah, thanks for that. I can feel the welt forming." He turns to Sophie. "Don't worry though, I got him back. As he was sprinting towards home, I threw the ball at his legs. You should've seen him trip and slide across the dirt."

That explains the blood.

Ryan reveals his scraped-up forearm. "Our little competition was a hit though. With every confrontation we had, the kids screamed in excitement."

Not sure that I should ask but can't help myself. "So, who won?"

"When the bell rang for dinner, the score was tied."

Jake rolls his neck. "Anyway, what were you saying about a secret?"

Sophie's face brightens, and she begins rambling off the story. "The librarian in town was excited to tell us about the signs. Shortly before World War II, a young immigrant from Germany named Hans moved here to find work. He heard there were jobs around Lake Superior, so he made his way here to Minnesota."

When she pauses for a breath, I take over the tale.

"He settled in that cute little town down the road and found a job stocking shelves at the local grocery store, befriending the owner's daughter, Isabelle. The town consisted mostly of Swedish immigrants and when the war began, they didn't trust the German boy. People were scared and took their fear out on Hans, banning him from entering restaurants and stores. Even Isabelle's father caved under the pressure and fired him."

Our tag-team story-telling makes it seem like we've been friends for years. Today was so much fun, perusing all the archives together. We may just have found our joint interest.

Sophie nods, then continues. "The local priest gave Hans shelter for a while but when the congregation began withholding donations, Hans left, not wanting the priest to suffer. Hans felt like everyone, including God, had turned against him and in his anger, he stole a gold cross from the altar."

"Like Jean Valjean," Jake says.

"You know, *Les Mis!*" I gasp. "It's one of my favorite Broadway shows. You like musicals? What's your favorite?"

Jake flinches, looking slightly scared. "No, sorry, I don't know too many plays. I read the book."

"Oh." Darn. Oh, well. "Anyway, back to the story.

Isabelle was heartbroken that Hans had fled. She began to avoid town and started taking long walks through the forest here. One day, Hans approached her. He had been hiding out in an old hunting cabin, living off the land. He felt guilty for stealing from the church and knew it was wrong but was hurt and confused."

When I pause, Sophie takes over again. "Isabelle and Hans eventually fell in love. One day on her way to meet him, two men traveling through the area grabbed Isabelle. Hans confronted them and saved Isabelle from the attack but was stabbed. Isabelle ran into town, pleading with everyone to help. No one would listen except for the priest. He went with her to the woods and found the dying boy. The priest offered the young man forgiveness before he died."

Jake cocks his head to the side. "What happened to the cross he stole from the church?"

"It was never found," Sophie explains. "But when the priest shared this story of sacrifice, love, and forgiveness in his homily, the community felt horrible for how they'd treated him, so they named all these trails and places in his honor. Even this camp." She pauses briefly as the story ends. "The librarian made us copies of the letters and Isabelle's diary."

I sigh, leaning against Ryan's shoulder. "Isn't that the most beautiful love story?"

Ryan shifts. "How have I never heard of this before? Do you think the gold is still hidden in these mountains somewhere?"

"Are you kidding?" I push his shoulder. "You hear the most romantic story ever and that's what pops into your mind?"

"Um, yeah." Ryan glances at Jake, who nods in agreement.

A mischievous grin slides onto Sophie's face. "Well, us too. The cross was never found. Seems we have a mystery on our hands."

WEDNESDAY

How can working with a gaggle of kids be so draining? Of course, my exhaustion might be because last night Sophie and I lay awake for hours reading the copies of Isabelle's journal and the letters between her and Hans.

Enjoying a brief reprieve from my duties while the kids are at chapel, I'm sitting under a tree near the lake, re-reading one of the letters and contemplating how their ill-fated relationship reminds me of other famous tragic love stories, when suddenly something plops into the lake. A huge splash sends drops of water raining down on me. Startled, I look up.

The culprit stands nearby, a mischievous grin plastered on his face. Jet.

Well, that's unexpected.

"I should warn you," I calmly tell him. "I have a little brother about your age, so I have many years of experience putting obnoxious boys in their place."

He eyes me warily. "I'm faster than you. There's no

way you can catch me."

"That might be true, but I'm patient and will strike when least expected."

His face crinkles as he contemplates my words. "Why are you out here all by yourself?"

"I could ask you the same question." His talkativeness is surprising; usually he's sulking around by himself.

"I asked you first."

"Fair enough. I'm reading some old letters."

"From who?"

"It's actually pretty interesting." I pat the ground next to me. "Want to hear about it?"

His eyebrows furrow, suspicion in his eyes, then slowly he approaches. Warily, he sits down, keeping his distance as if he thinks I might have cooties or something.

For the next twenty minutes, he quietly listens as I tell him about Isabelle and Hans and all the places around camp named after them.

"Did he ever return the cross?" He runs his fingers through the grass.

I cringe at the dirt that's caked under his nails. "No. It might still be hidden around here somewhere."

"Cool. What happened to those two? Did they do something stupid like get married?"

I can't help but smile. "No."

Reluctantly, I tell him about the tragic ending to Isabelle and Hans' story.

"Seriously? That's a dumb ending."

"Totally. Although, when the town eventually heard

how he saved her and apologized for stealing the cross, they all felt horrible for the way they'd treated him. So, to honor him, they named the sites after the two of them. It's actually a beautiful story of forgiveness."

He looks at me, his face full of questions. "But why would he do that? Sacrifice himself for her?"

"Because he loved her."

He rolls his eyes. "Love makes you do dumb things."

I laugh. "Yeah, that's pretty much the definition of love. But seriously, risking everything to protect those you care about is pure love." A thought pops into my mind. "Like when Jesus sacrificed Himself for us."

When his eyes glaze over, I know I've gone too far. Darn it.

In one quick move, he jumps up but doesn't leave like I expected him to. Instead he walks towards the edge of the lake, kicking everything in his path, grass, flowers, rocks, dirt.

What makes this little pigpen tick? And how are any of us ever going to reach him? We're running out of time.

I join him by the water, hoping to somehow connect with him. "I've noticed you never join in at any of the field games."

"I don't really like sports." He picks up a pinecone and flings it into the lake.

"Yeah, I can relate to not doing the whole sports thing. Every time I've tried has ended up in disaster."

His dark eyes peer at me from beneath his veil of greasy bangs. "Disaster?"

I nod. "A scraped knee during tennis, a twisted ankle in basketball, a mild concussion when the softball I was trying to catch hit my head instead of my mitt. Oh, and then there was the time I tried soccer and slid into a patch of clover and was stung by a bee."

A slight grin forms on his face. "You're kinda accident prone."

"Yep, that's me. But then I got interested in theater. I liked the acting, singing, and even the dancing. It was great to finally find something I was good at. So, what are you good at?"

He looks back at his feet. "I guess music's kinda cool."

Shocked that he actually answered, I nod. "Yeah, music is pretty awesome. It can be a great way to forget about problems for a while too."

One grimy sneaker kicks the dirt, creating a swirling cloud of dust around him. "Exactly."

As the air clears, his gaze shifts from my face to something behind me. Immediately his demeanor changes. His hands sink into his pockets and his shoulders stiffen.

I turn around to see Ryan, Jake, and Sophie coming towards us.

"Hey, mind if we join you?" Ryan sets down the large backpack that he's carrying.

"It's a free country," Jet sasses back.

Sophie ignores his rudeness and reaches down to grab a flat stone. "Jet, do you know how to skip rocks?"

His face softens—slightly. "What's that?"

"Here, I'll show you. One summer, our grandpa

showed Ryan and me how to do it."

She zings the stone towards the water. It makes three hops across the smooth surface before sinking.

Jet's eyes widen.

Soon we're all scouring the shore for smooth flat stones.

"Here, Sophie." Ryan offers her one. "Here's a good one for you."

She reaches out to grab the large stone.

"AKK!" She pulls her hand back as a little leg wiggles out from the side of the stone.

Poor, innocent little turtle.

Jet crumples in a fit of laughter.

"Don't worry," she tells him. "Ryan might have struck first but I'll get him back."

As sorry as I feel for the turtle getting caught up in one of Ryan and Sophie's pranks, seeing Jet having fun is the best thing I've seen all day.

Soon we're all immersed in a competition to see who can skip their rock the furthest. My stones always just sink to the bottom, but everyone else seems to have perfected the skill.

When the lunch bell rings, Jet waves good-bye and scurries towards the dining hall. A smile still on his face.

"Shall we join him?" I brush off my hands.

Sophie shakes her head. "No, we've got a better plan. The cook let me pack a picnic. I thought we could all go on a hike, unless of course the boys are tired of hiking after their morning outing with the campers."

Jake drapes his arm around her shoulder. "Hiking with

you girls shouldn't be as difficult as hiking with thirty rug rats."

That's what he thinks. "You haven't hiked too much with me yet. I've had a few interesting incidents."

"She speaks the truth." Ryan hitches the backpack onto his shoulder. "Where to?"

The perfect place comes to mind. "Well, we could check out the spots that Isabelle mentions in her diary. Maybe we'll get lucky and find the hidden cross."

Before long, our leisurely stroll is ruined when the guys decide to race each other to the clearing at the end of the trail, leaving us in the dust.

Sophie shakes her head as they take off. "Those two are a little too alike."

"I know. They've been competing in everything this week. We should make a bet on which one will get injured first."

"They'd probably turn that into a competition as well." She pushes a low-hanging branch out of her way. "You know, I can't stop thinking about Hans and Isabelle."

"Me either. It's been fun reading the journal and letters with you."

She turns to me, her eyes meeting mine, then smiles. "Yeah, it has been fun. I keep thinking how their story reminds me of one of the great love stories. Like Gatsby and Daisy."

"That's what I've been thinking! Our very own Lancelot and Guinevere."

By the time we reach the clearing that Isabelle wrote

about in her journal, a large field of wildflowers surrounded by tall, twisted oaks, Ryan and Jake have a spot picked out for our picnic.

"Isabelle brought Hans here for picnics of their own." I begin pulling the food from the backpack. "Isn't that so romantic?"

Ryan grabs the bag of chips. "You two are getting a little obsessed with this story."

"That's because it's a beautiful story." Sophie reaches for the sandwich I hand her. "Isabelle saw a side to him that no one else saw. She wanted to prove to him that not everyone was cruel. She thought if he returned the cross and came back to town, she could convince people they were wrong about him. But he didn't think that was possible. In her diary, she wrote that after he died, she went back to the cabin and found a note he'd written her. It's a bit vague but sounds a little like a goodbye note."

"See, this is not one of your romance novels. Real life doesn't always have happy endings." Jake leans back on his elbows.

"Yeah, I wish they could've lived happily ever after." Sophie takes a bite of her sandwich.

I shake my head. "But in a way, I think their story did have a happy ending."

"He's dead. And no one ever found the treasure. That's your idea of a happy ending?" Ryan asks.

I throw a grape at his head. "It's clear that she did reach him. He knew she loved him. But he also realized he couldn't stay here, that there was no future for the two of them. I don't think he planned to sell the gold. I've been re-reading his last letter. It sounds like a goodbye note, but I think it's also a clue."

"A clue?" Jake reaches for his water bottle.

"I think it might be a hint to where he left the cross." Excitement bubbling up inside me, I pull out the letter. "Listen. He wrote, 'All the gold in the world cannot mend the deep chasm created by a broken heart, but finding it can create a new life.' Isn't that beautiful?"

Sophie leans forward. "Now that you mention it, it does sound rather cryptic."

"If it's a clue, where's this chasm?" Jake asks.

"That, I don't know. Nothing we've seen so far matches that description. After lunch we could check out the remaining places marked by those signs."

We spend the next hour exploring the area but don't see anything that looks like a chasm.

We're on our way back to camp when we pass by a small pool at the base of a waterfall. My foot slips on the mossy rock, and next thing I know, I'm in the water, my head popping to the surface.

"I think you got a little too close." Ryan laughs as he leans over and offers his hand to help me out.

As I reach for him, Sophie catches my eye. I read her mind and move out of the way. In one quick move, she shoves him into the pond. She and I pretend to high-five to celebrate her retaliation.

THURSDAY

While the boys are back at camp with the kids, Sophie and I are exploring the last few Hans and Isabelle locations. Our time here is winding down.

In one of the quiet moments of our conversation, we hear it. A muffled cry.

"Help."

We look at each other.

"Where's that coming from?" I latch onto her arm.

She shakes her head. "I don't know."

"Help! Help!!"

Racing through the forest, we follow the pleas for help. The call reverberates around the rocks, making it hard to pinpoint.

The good news is I only have one mishap as we frantically search—a scraped-up knee after tripping over a fallen tree. The better news is that my scream scared away any lurking wildlife. And the best news is that when we burst through the woods, coming upon the tall rocky formation we had dubbed Sophie's Stonehenge a few days ago, we find our person in need. Huddled against the base of the two large boulders sits Jet.

I stand staring at him, my hand squeezing my aching side. "What're you doing out here by yourself?"

"Exploring." Tears streak his filthy face.

"Are you hurt?" I kneel next to him.

"My foot's caught."

I lean over to examine the situation. His right foot is

wedged between two smaller boulders. I push on them, but they don't budge.

"Will they have to cut off my foot?" Panic fills Jet's eyes.

I reach for his dusty hand. "Don't worry, you'll be fine. We need some help though."

"Don't leave me," Jet pleads, clamping onto me.

Sophie smiles at the frightened boy. "Don't worry, Josie will stay here with you. I'll go get Ryan and Jake."

After a nod of encouragement, she disappears through the trees.

Jet sniffs. "Thanks for staying. Most people end up leaving me."

I pull him into a hug. "Jet, you know your brother didn't want to leave you, right?"

"He still did."

I glance at his foot. All week I've been praying that someone would be able to reach him; now he's stuck and can't leave. Maybe God provided this golden opportunity for me to talk with him.

"Do you think your brother would be happy that you're not taking full advantage of the opportunities given to you, like the chance to come to this camp?"

He pushes me away. "I'm here ain't I?"

"True, but you're not really making the most of it. Your brother was working hard to give you a brighter future. Maybe you could honor him by doing more with your life."

"But I can't stop being angry," he quietly admits.

"I know, but you've got to find a way to forgive, or the

anger will consume you."

The glare I receive is as poisonous as Romeo's potion.

"*Forgive*? Forgive the people who killed my brother?"

Please God, give me the right words.

"Yes. If Jesus forgave the people who killed Him, we can forgive, too. Give your burdens to God. I know about holding onto anger and, believe me, it'll destroy you. And then those men will have killed both you and your brother. You have a chance to live your life for the two of you and make a real difference."

He runs his fingers through the dirt. "You make it sound easy, but you don't have to go back to my neighborhood."

He's got a point. "Do you think we could keep in touch? You could call and text when you need someone to talk to. We all need friends to help us through the rough times. Ryan helped me once, and now I can help you."

His little shoulders rise and fall in a shrug.

I lean into him. "I believe we all have unique talents from God. You said you like music. Maybe there's some way we can use that to help you get out of that neighborhood. I mean, you could learn to be a DJ or be in a band or something. Do you play any instruments?"

His eyebrows furrow as he stares at the ground. "Well, kinda."

I stare at him. "Really? That's great. Too bad you didn't bring it. We could've put you in my amazing talent show."

The edge of his mouth turns up into a slight grin.

Soon Sophie appears, followed by Jake and Ryan. "Found them in the middle of a very intense game of ping-pong."

"I was winning." Ryan pats himself on the shoulder.

Jake shoves him aside. "By one point. I call for a re-match."

Sophie rolls her eyes and walks towards us. "Can you two stop competing for one moment and come help us move this rock?"

After assessing the best course of action, Ryan and Jake push against the smaller of the boulders. After the third attempt, the rock shifts enough for Jet to pull his foot out.

I gently examine his ankle. "I still don't get what you were doing up here by yourself."

"I kept thinking about those dumb love letters you showed me. That guy mentioned the giant heartbreak, and it made me think of this rock formation."

All eyes travel to the two huge rocks jutting out from the earth. The boulders both start out narrow at the base and widen toward the middle. Their slightly rounded tops give them a bit of a heart shape, a narrow crevice between them breaking the heart in two.

"Whoa," Sophie whispers.

"What did Hans say about the broken heart again?" Ryan asks.

"*All the gold in the world can't mend the deep chasm created by a broken heart, but finding it can create a new life.*" Sophie impressively recites the words from memory.

Jet shoots us a mischievous grin and then reaches between the two rocks that make the heart shape. He stretches his arm far into the space, plastering his face against the rock.

"Careful!" I yell. "We don't want you to get your hand caught this time."

"I feel something! But I can't reach it."

"Here, let me try," Sophie offers.

She moves into position and reaches into the dark crevice.

"Jet's right. There's something here, some sort of cloth." She strains to reach a little further. Her face scrunches then she pulls out a wrapped bundle and hands it to Jet.

"Since you're the one who had the idea to check here, you should be the one to open it."

His wide eyes and shocked expression transform into a huge smile as he takes the bundle from her and slowly unwraps the dirty material. The cloth crumbles apart revealing a leather pouch. Jet drops the disintegrating rags and opens the pouch. He pulls out a cross, sunlight highlighting the intricately-carved details.

"Wow!" I cling to Ryan's arm.

Sophie hugs Jet. "This is amazing!"

"Way to go, little dude." Ryan messes up Jet's wild hair.

I smile at his beaming face, which is more precious than the beautiful gold cross. "You did it, you figured out the secret no one else has ever been able to solve!"

FRIDAY

After a chaotic day of interviews with the police, mayor, and local newspaper, the excitement of Jet's discovery has died down a little. Now it's time for the big event. The talent show.

From the side of the stage, I look out to see Ryan, Sophie, and Jake sitting with the kids in the audience.

When the first strains of "Food Glorious Food" from the musical *Oliver* fill the room, the kids take the stage and attempt the choreography we've been rehearsing all week. They are so cute. Not sure any of them have a future in musical theater, but they do a great job.

One by one, I introduce the talent show contestants. One brave fellow tries a stand-up comedy routine. Another boy burps the alphabet. Two girls dance to a popular hip-hop song. When one of the little girls stands frozen in place, staring at the audience, I join her, and we sing her song as a duet.

After the last planned act, I take center stage once again. "We have one final act this evening. While I set it up, will you all please help me encourage Ryan to come up on stage?" I hold out three oranges to him.

I hadn't told him my plan but knew he wouldn't mind. He shoots a grin towards Sophie. She starts laughing as he comes on stage and begins his juggling act.

Once he'd told me why he had learned to juggle. It was years ago, after Sophie informed him she wasn't going to attend their annual summer trip because she was going to circus school to become a trapeze artist. He believed her and, not wanting to be alone on the vacation with the adults and their younger siblings, he spent months teaching himself to juggle so he could be admitted into circus school as well.

The audience *oohs* and *aahs* at his impressive tricks. Assured everything is set behind the curtain, I come back to the side of the stage and watch as he ends the routine by tossing the oranges to kids in the audience. Then he bows.

When the applause dies down, everyone's eyes turn to me.

"Before we end tonight, I'm excited to announce that we have a surprise last-minute performance." With dramatic flourish, I pull back the curtain. The crowd murmurs in surprise as they slowly recognize the clean boy with slicked back hair, sitting at the piano in the center of the stage. Jet.

His huge round eyes stare at me. I smile and nod. Then he begins to play.

The notes come out quietly at first as he tentatively hits the keys. Then his shoulders relax, and he focuses on the song. The music that pours from this troubled boy is incredible. When he told me he wanted to play tonight I had no idea that this boy, so full of hurt and fear, was a musical genius. I guess more than one secret was discovered this week.

When he finishes, the room remains silent for a moment. Then everyone leaps up in a heartfelt ovation. Jet's eyes glisten with tears as he scans the applauding crowd. He beams at the genuine love and admiration. Somehow, I know he's going to be okay.

Thanks, God.

This short story combines the lead characters from two of Leslea Wahl's award-winning Catholic YA novels. Jake and Sophie's exciting story about finding and using your gifts from God, can be found in *The Perfect Blindside*, a first-place winner of a 2016 Catholic Press Association Award, as well as a 2016 Silver Medal Illumination Christian Book Award. Josie and Ryan's adventurous tale about finding who God wants you to be, is titled *An Unexpected Role*, and is a recipient of a 2017 Gold Medal Moonbeam Children's Book Award.

Leslea Wahl

ABOUT THE AUTHOR

LESLEA WAHL lives in beautiful Colorado with her husband and children. The furry, four-legged members of her family often make cameo appearances in her novels. Leslea's writing career began when she was searching for faith-inspired books for her own children and the idea for her first novel popped into her head. That divine inspiration has led to a successful writing ministry that she hopes encourages teens to grow in their faith through fun adventures. For more information about her faith-filled young adult mysteries, visit www.LesleaWahl.com.

BOOKS FOR TEENS & YOUNG ADULTS
BY THESE AUTHORS

CAROLYN ASTFALK
Rightfully Ours

T.M. GAOUETTE
The Destiny Of Sunshine Ranch
Freeing Tanner Rose
Saving Faith

THERESA LINDEN
Roland West, Loner
Life-Changing Love
Battle For His Soul
Standing Strong
Chasing Liberty
Testing Liberty
Fight For Liberty

SUSAN PEEK
A Soldier Surrenders:
The Conversion of St. Camillus de Lellis
Crusader King:
A Novel of Baldwin IV and the Crusades
Saint Magnus, the Last Viking
The King's Prey:
Saint Dymphna of Ireland

CYNTHIA T. TONEY
8 Notes To A Nobody
10 Steps To Girlfriend Status
6 Dates To Disaster
The Other Side Of Freedom

CORINNA TURNER
I Am Margaret
The Three Most Wanted
Liberation
Bane's Eyes
Margo's Diary
Brothers
Someday
Drive! (Unsparked 1.0)
Elfling
Mandy Lamb and the Full Moon

LESLEA WAHL
The Perfect Blindside
An Unexpected Role
Where You Lead

Visit CatholicTeenBooks.com for even more authors and titles.

And subscribe to our newsletter for new titles
hot off the press!